Elaine Leong Eng, MD

"Martha, Martha"
How Christians Worry

*Pre-publication
REVIEWS,
COMMENTARIES,
EVALUATIONS . . .*

"This is a very helpful book about the 'secret suffering' of persons with conditions such as obsessive-compulsive disorder, panic disorder, and post-traumatic stress disorder. In direct, simple language Dr. Eng offers cogent explanations and descriptions of these and other conditions along with strategies for addressing them. Dr. Eng brings her biblically rooted faith perspective into conversations with her medical and psychiatric expertise. The result is a volume of considerable practical value for those engaged in counseling and referral. This book is particularly useful in the way it describes various treatments and therapies, especially behavioral approaches and medication. It might also be an ex-cellent resource for those planning retreats, lay ministry training, and adult education classes in a congregational setting.

Dr. Eng effectively advocates for an enlightened approach to caring for those who otherwise might live their lives in mental darkness. Her book deserves the attention of clergy, denominational leaders, and laypersons; in short all those who are interested in alleviating the stigma of mental illness and providing pastoral care of the highest quality."

Reverend Curtis W. Hart, MDiv
Director of Pastoral Care
and Education,
New York Presbyterian Hospital—
New York Weill Cornell Center,
New York, NY

"**D**r. Eng has produced a valuable handbook for Christians—a manual of basic information about psychiatric anxiety disorders and how such disorders may impact the lives of believers. The interested reader will learn that there are various ways to worry, that Christians may suffer from any of them, and that in most cases effective treatment is available. Is such a handbook needed? It certainly is. As a clinical psychologist I have encountered patients who have been counseled and/or medicated for years—for the wrong disorder. Such tragedies need not continue to occur. In the hands of counselors, pastors, and clients themselves, Dr. Eng's book can help prevent such errors as, for example, failing to correctly diagnose obsessive-compulsive disorders when, at last, effective specific behavioral and pharmacological treatments have become available. In the same way, the various anxiety disorders are presented with clarity, enabling nonclinicians to understand their own form of worry and the most effective current treatments.

For helpers, their clients, and individuals who are worried about their worrying, as well as for their friends and relatives, Dr. Eng's book can be a most useful guide."

William Backus, PhD
Licensed Psychologist;
Author, *Telling Yourself the Truth*
and *The Healing Power
of the Christian Mind,*
St. Paul, MN

"**D**r. Elaine Leong Eng has provided the Christian community with a valuable resource for understanding and treating the many aspects of worry. She carefully educates the reader about the complexities involved, from 'simple' worry to debilitating anxiety, depression, and other problems. Unique to this book is the way in which the author brings the Christian community into the picture. Taking a very positive approach, she assumes that hurting people in the Christian community have resources right next to them on a daily basis—their family and fellow Christians. She gives specific help to these people on how to understand their struggles, find resources, and maintain healthy attitudes in their daily lives.

This book is a rich resource for the church. Pastors and other workers can use it as a tool to help them understand some of their more troubled parishioners. Hurting people themselves can use this book to guide them to healthy choices they need to make. Family and Christian friends can find a wealth of information to help them in their task of 'loving one another'!"

Brent Lindquist, PhD
President,
Link Care Center,
Fresno, CA

"**T**his very thoughtful, encouraging, and practical book is a much-needed synthesis of Christian belief with psychiatric diagnosis and treatment—without compromising either one. As Dr. Eng presents each case study as an introduction to different psychiatric disorders, she draws readers in and encourages them to look around their own lives to see people who may have similar struggles. She explains different facets of psychiatric illness in a manner that brings clarity and focus to often confusing behavior. Once she has captured our empathy, she provides very practical guidelines for each of us to intervene appropriately so that opportunities for healing and wholeness may be optimized.

Dr. Eng affirms the sacredness and importance of each person within the church and within the larger society. In this affirmation, she challenges us to reject our own complacent and selfish behaviors in dealing with those with mental illness. We each choose to contribute to the problem or the solution and are the poorer or the richer for our choice.

Dr. Eng demonstrates a clear understanding of both Christian beliefs and psychiatric disease, and how the two interface. This book is an excellent culmination of her own experience in treating patients with the eyes of faith and the well-honed skills of psychiatric practice."

Lorraine A. Milio, MD
Assistant Professor,
Department of Gynecology
and Obstetrics,
Johns Hopkins University
Medical Center,
Baltimore, MD

"**A** valuable primer on anxiety, *Martha, Martha* is a fascinating, biblically sound, psychiatrically comprehensive, and practical book that Christian clergy and laity will find both applicable and helpful. Dr. Eng helps the reader to see an old biblical story through the windows of a malady that afflicts many inside and outside the church. Then she provides many tangible resources and suggestions for help."

Craig W. Ellison, PhD
Professor of Counseling,
Alliance Theological Seminary,
Nyack, NY

More pre-publication
REVIEWS, COMMENTARIES, EVALUATIONS . . .

"**F**ear or worry in their various forms are the most common reasons that people fail to enjoy life to the fullest. Committed Christians are no exception. In spite of receiving the free blessings of forgiveness and spiritual power, many believers still experience a severe lack of peace and joy in their lives. To such sufferers Dr. Eng offers emotional reassurance, realistic optimism, and practical guidance.

These pages describe the several different forms of anxiety and depression to which we are all so vulnerable. Dr. Eng encourages us to seek the professional help that God has provided in Christian doctors and therapists together with many scriptural exhortations of hope. She thoroughly embraces the integration of psychological wisdom, medical treatment, and biblical inspiration in the process of healing.

Dr. Eng deserves our gratitude and thanks for this uplifting gift to all those in need."

O. Quentin Hyder, MD, MDiv
Consulting Psychiatrist
to the Redeemer Counseling Service,
New York, NY

"**T**he author has shown a light into the dark corners of the Christian understanding of mental illness. Specifically, she takes readers through the gamut of anxiety disorders, helping them to identify, empathize with, and refer the sufferer to professional help without casting a judgmental or stigmatizing opinion. Surely, Jesus who told us to love our neighbors would want us to understand these brethren and their situations so that we could be of help to them. This book teaches both lay people and professionals to enter into the lonely and often misunderstood world of the anxious. Some Christians might ask how believers can be tormented by these conditions. Dr. Eng shows us how to recognize, understand, and support these individuals—BRAVO."

Christian S. Nahas, DO
Board-Certified Family Physician
and Assistant Professor
of Family Medicine,
New York Institute of Technology
at the New York School
of Osteopathic Medicine,
New York, NY

The Haworth Pastoral Press
An Imprint of The Haworth Press, Inc.

"Martha, Martha"
How Christians Worry

THE HAWORTH PASTORAL PRESS
Religion and Mental Health
Harold G. Koenig, MD
Senior Editor

New, Recent, and Forthcoming Titles:

A Gospel for the Mature Years: Finding Fulfillment by Knowing and Using Your Gifts by Harold Koenig, Tracy Lamar, and Betty Lamar

Is Religion Good for Your Health? The Effects of Religion on Physical and Mental Health by Harold Koenig

Adventures in Senior Living: Learning How to Make Retirement Meaningful and Enjoyable by J. Lawrence Driskill

Dying, Grieving, Faith, and Family: A Pastoral Care Approach by George W. Bowman

The Pastoral Care of Depression: A Guidebook by Binford W. Gilbert

Understanding Clergy Misconduct in Religious Systems: Scapegoating, Family Secrets, and the Abuse of Power by Candace R. Benyei

What the Dying Teach Us: Lessons on Living by Samuel Lee Oliver

The Pastor's Family: The Challenges of Family Life and Pastoral Responsibilities by Daniel L. Langford

Somebody's Knocking at Your Door: AIDS and the African-American Church by Ronald Jeffrey Weatherford and Carole Boston Weatherford

Grief Education for Caregivers of the Elderly by Junietta Baker McCall

The Obsessive-Compulsive Disorder: Pastoral Care for the Road to Change by Robert M. Collie

The Pastoral Care of Children by David H. Grossoehme

Ways of the Desert: Becoming Holy Through Difficult Times by William F. Kraft

Caring for a Loved One with Alzheimer's Disease: A Christian Perspective by Elizabeth T. Hall

"Martha, Martha": How Christians Worry by Elaine Leong Eng

Spiritual Care for Children Living in Specialized Settings: Breathing Underwater by Michael F. Friesen

Broken Bodies, Healing Hearts: Reflections of a Hospital Chaplain by Gretchen W. TenBrook

"Martha, Martha"
How Christians Worry

Elaine Leong Eng, MD

The Haworth Pastoral Press
An Imprint of The Haworth Press, Inc.
New York • London • Oxford

Published by

The Haworth Pastoral Press, an imprint of The Haworth Press, Inc., 10 Alice Street, Binghamton, NY 13904-1580

Cover design by Marylouise E. Doyle.

Scripture taken from the *Holy Bible, New International Version.* Copyright © 1973, 1978, 1984 by International Bible Society. Used by permission of Zondervan Bible Publishers.

Library of Congress Cataloging-in-Publication Data

Eng, Elaine Leong.
    Martha, Martha: how Christians worry / Elaine Leong Eng.
       p.   cm.
    Includes bibliographical references and index.
    ISBN 0-7890-0865-3 (hard) — ISBN 0-7890-0866-1 (pbk.)
    1. Anxiety—Religious aspects—Christianity. I. Title.
BV4908.5 E64 2000
248.8′62--dc21
                                                CIP
                                             99-039460

This book is dedicated to
Clifford, Brian, and Genevieve

ABOUT THE AUTHOR

Elaine Leong Eng, MD, is Assistant Professor of Psychiatry in the Department of Obstetrics and Gynecology at Cornell University—Weill Medical College, New York City. She received a BA in Biology and a Certificate in the Program of Science and Human Affairs from Princeton University. Dr. Eng is board certified by the American Board of Psychiatry and Neurology, and she was trained at the Lay Ministry program of Concordia College. She is Vice President of the Board of Directors at the Boro Pregnancy Counseling Center and maintains a private practice in New York. Dr. Eng's professional interests include mental health education for the church community and the treatment of anxiety disorders. Because of her background in obstetrics/gynecology and psychiatry, she specializes in the treatment of women with psychiatric conditions related to issues of reproduction such as menopause, premenstrual syndrome, postpartum depression, perinatal grief, and infertility. Speaking engagements on cable television, radio, church conferences, and professional meetings have been avenues for Dr. Eng to provide information in her areas of expertise. Dr. Eng has authored journal articles and has also reviewed books for the *Journal of Religion and Health.*

CONTENTS

Foreword

Here is a lucid and gentle work that deserves to be, and should be, read by all Christians who have a true concern for the effectiveness and inclusiveness of their ministry. A true "Christian psychiatrist" writes it. People seeking help often ask, with apology, for a Christian psychiatrist. They are seeking some kind of reassurance as they ambivalently seek assistance. Only a little over a century ago, mental illness was often viewed as the work of the devil, or a punishment for sinful behavior. Those attempting to understand, let alone heal, such stricken individuals, were also seen as questionable individuals to be shunned by the God fearing. Indeed, in the nineteenth century, psychiatrists were called "alienists."

The divide between psychiatry and religion widened with the advent of Freud's theories about the basis of mental illness. His works such as *The Future of an Illusion* obscured, for many religious people, the momentous contributions he made toward understanding the workings of the mind. The biological concept of "mind" must be kept separate from the religious concept of "spirit" as good people attempt to close this unreasonable divide between religion and psychiatric practice.

Of course, in this book Dr. Eng is not attempting to fit her worrying Christian friends into a Freudian mold. Yet, my fear is that many who could benefit from the kind and soft wisdom of Dr. Eng will be put off by the feeling that their suffering is shameful or sinful and they cannot turn for help from alien or atheistic practitioners. Dr. Eng is just the person to close the gap and bring help to the suffering souls. She is a devoted Christian and a brilliant and well-schooled psychiatrist. I believe that her credentials on both sides are impeccable!

So, let us turn to the words and methods of Dr. Eng as she uses her well-informed and well-intentioned professionalism to foster the best growth of her Christian colleagues to better serve their present and potential ministrants. She begins with a well-chosen and likely collection of examples any of us could, and have, encountered in our daily comings and goings. The contradictory and puzzling behaviors that are the presenting wedge of the troubled mind are the natural starting point. Dr. Eng clearly and empathetically portrays these behaviors. Each chapter begins with an air of mystery, and some surprise. The worries and concerns are soon pulled together with understanding.

The discussion sections that immediately follow the opening example provide the richest examples of Dr. Eng's synthetic abilities. She skillfully interweaves insightful professional understanding of each "worry" with scriptural quotes directed toward the same issue. Conflict disappears as the discourse unfolds. Both the Bible and the psychiatrist are saying the same things, without contradiction, albeit from a different perspective and using different language. The result is a much-needed synthesis of the two disciplines to serve the worried Christian in a better and total manner.

The author then goes into a series of very useful directives to those Christians attempting to truly help those suffering. The advice is based on sound professional understanding and description, with explanations any layperson can easily understand. Directives to the helping person are clear and nonjudgmental. One need not feel at sea and awash with confusion as we are guided toward simple understanding and consequent action.

Where can I learn more about this? Dr. Eng hears this question and she provides a good database of resources, both to understand mental disorders and to seek help for them.

This book is a most welcome and well-done entry into an area that has long languished in alienation. Religion and psychiatry should be allies, rather than antagonists. Both disciplines are seeking the same goals. To paraphrase Isaiah: We must seek understanding fairly, dedicate ourselves to helping, and remain humble in our efforts before God.

Thornton A. Vandersall
Emeritus Professor of Clinical Psychiatry
Cornell University Medical College

Acknowledgments

I am sincerely grateful for the leadership, wisdom, and encouragement of Dr. Thornton Vandersall in influencing my career in psychiatry and ultimately in the formulation of this book. I also wish to thank Dr. Craig Ellison, Dr. Walter Byrd, Ms. Maymay Quey Lin, Dr. Tara Dill, Dr. Lucia Brandao, Dr. Junko Tanaka-Matsumi, Dr. Gerald Cohen, Dr. Bruce Ballard, Ms. Helen Yu, Dr. Jennifer Downey, Reverend Lee Hearn, and members of P.A.L.M. (Pastoral and Laity Ministries) for their thoughtful assistance in the preparation of the manuscript.

Introduction:
"Worried and Upset"

Why name a book after Martha? Although a prominent woman in the new testament, she does not possess the worthy position of the Virgin Mary or reflect the matured spirituality of an Elizabeth. In fact in many Sunday sermons, she is maligned as being the only one of two sisters who forsook the opportunity to learn from the teachings of a master so she could attend to what was in essence, household chores. "Don't be a Martha," we are admonished. Hence, this book is written to put Martha's name in its proper perspective. Although she is memorialized for this one transgression, her real strengths and contributions to the lives of her peers require emphasis. Martha, by virtue of her faith, hard work, and hospitality was a pillar of that early religious community in Bethany. The impetus for this book comes from clinical experience with many patients who resemble the biblical figure Martha. With excellent track records of performance in their church, they then become derailed and are filled with anxiety. Negotiating this turn of events is not only an important task for the individual "Martha," but it is ultimately shared with the church. This book is written to equip those concerned with the restoration of these faithful, talented individuals The description of Martha's worried state is well depicted in Luke 10:38-42.[1]

> As Jesus and his disciples were on their way, he came to a village where a woman named Martha opened her home to him. She had a sister called Mary, who sat at the Lord's feet listening to what he said. But Martha was distracted by all the preparations that had to be made. She came to him and

asked, "Lord, don't you care that my sister has left me to do the work by myself? Tell her to help me!"

"Martha, Martha," the Lord answered, "You are worried and upset about many things, but only one thing is needed. Mary has chosen what is better, and it will not be taken away from her."

The passage states that Martha is worried and upset about many things. Her worries began after she extended an invitation to the Lord to come to her house, which she appeared to do wholeheartedly. However, anxiety took hold and instead of sitting at the Lord's feet she became distracted about the preparations and worried about much. The Lord indicates that Mary has chosen what is better, implying that Martha had the same choice. Although not intuitive, to worry or not to worry is often a choice. Most of us would obviously choose not to worry following the counsel found in Philippians 4:6, "Do not be anxious about anything, but in everything, by prayer and petition, with thanksgiving, present your requests to God."[2] However, at times, people admit that they have difficulty heeding this Scripture despite its authenticity and truth.

Living in this age of anxiety, there may be many reasons why Christians worry. Real life stressors can impact our lives. Yet worry in its most overshadowing and consuming form does not yield any benefits. It is in this context that one should claim the choice, choosing not to worry versus choosing to worry. How can one make the choice? There are multiple ways. Mary, in the gospel account, chose simply to sit at the Lord's feet and listen to His teachings. This is a time-honored method and has been proven to be an effective anxiety-relieving strategy for many. Some people may have to deal with psychological reasons such as personal conflicts or learned misperceptions of the world. This makes it difficult for them to sit down at the Lord's feet and simply listen. Martha's worries and distractions prevented her from listening to Jesus in a receptive manner.

Some may be suffering from a medical condition in which anxiety is a prominent feature. Discerning the causes of anxiety may be quite difficult. One finds that this is true in the church setting as well as in society. Yet, these people require the sensitive help of family, friends, ministers, educational resources, books, or professional counseling.

It is my hope that this book will identify and help the many "Marthas" within your community. It contains the narratives of fictional composites of potentially real people. This manner of illustration is designed to improve your recognition of people afflicted with what is called anxiety disorders. These are conditions in which fear and anxiety have gone haywire.

Ordinarily, fear and anxiety are normal human responses to threatening situations and prepare a person for fight or flight. They can also sharpen a person for action and are in many cases adaptive. Anxiety disorders do not refer to this normal human response but rather to illnesses that are reflected by anxiety gone awry. Chapters on depression and premenstrual syndrome are also included because many people who suffer from these problems may have anxiety as the main complaint.

Most of the narratives are descriptive of the sufferer but others are written from the point of view of a fellow church member in the first person. The latter is an attempt to draw the reader into the predicaments experienced by other congregants. A certain amount of discomfort will have to be tolerated by the reader in order to learn from the text. In a community and a society where mental health issues tend to be misunderstood, stigmatized, and avoided, tolerating the tension may be no simple request. However, it is worthwhile to persevere and learn in order to help our "Marthas." These are people who not only have the capacity to function, but are often the "doers," if not the pillars of the church. These men and women need to be appreciated for the roles they play in the body of Christ. They often carry on very useful lives at home or at work. But at times this is disrupted when they are plagued with worries caused by their condition. Unfortunately, it may also interfere with their relationships or their ministries.

Recognizing these individuals and helping to care for them will ultimately help the church. These vital church figures are struggling with a real problem. Understanding the psychiatric causes of severe anxiety will help the church leader, pastoral counselor, seminary student, or caring individual to have a keen understanding and sensitivity toward the "Marthas" in the church. One will also learn to direct sufferers to obtain professional care when indicated.

This book is an educational tool. It does not intend to give the biblical figure Martha a psychiatric diagnosis nor should readers conclude that they can make diagnostic judgments of their congregations. It is intended to broaden the church's understanding of the psychiatric factors causing anxiety, which is a topic neglected in the religious library. In my work, I have seen many anxious patients who have benefited from treatment and resume their active services in their church. The goal of this book is to educate readers in helping these people find the means to overcome their anxiety and to continue serving the Lord, as the biblical Martha did throughout the New Testament account.

Chapter 1

Obsessions and Compulsions

Marianne, a middle-aged schoolteacher, worshipped in a large church in a metropolitan area. She was quite active in her church, working in the areas of evangelism and ministries to the homeless. She enjoyed a successful career as a schoolteacher and the respect of her fellow church members for her ability to teach Sunday school, to organize activities, and to be of encouragement to those who were suffering. Little did anyone know that Marianne was suffering as well. Marianne had always known that she had quirky, eccentric ways since she was a child. She would often be bound to certain "habits" such as "not stepping on a crack because I'll break my parent's back." Although many children play this game, Marianne's mother always felt that her daughter took it to an extreme. Marianne would refuse to veer from this rule and was often late getting to school. When her mother tried to stop her, she would become very anxious and upset. She also had to have her toys organized symmetrically or she would not be comfortable. Although Marianne did reasonably well in school, earning top grades and developing a few friendships, she remained quite an anxious child and was fearful of new situations. After marriage, she blossomed and became very active socially and in her church.

The pastor always welcomed Marianne into his committee meetings. She had a flair and an enthusiasm for the Lord's work that seemed to encourage him when he felt somewhat discouraged. One day Marianne approached him to discuss her fears about a particular church project. She told him that she was worried the program might not get under way without the help of a large number of people and that she felt doubtful about her ability to handle the task. She hinted that she was constantly praying for direction from God but felt she wasn't getting answers no matter how hard she prayed. She felt quite anxious and hoped that she could meet again with the pastor on this matter.

At the next meeting, Marianne, who was never a prompt person, arrived quite late and apologized saying that she could not get out of the house on time, vaguely mumbling that there was so much to do. She presented a long list of items that needed to be done on the project and remarked that she had worked all week on this list checking and rechecking it for its completeness. The pastor looked at it and pondered. This project although important, did not warrant the kind of worry and scrutiny that Marianne seemed to give it. In addition, the list, although adequate, did not reflect the number of hours that Marianne had poured into it. He thanked her for her work and puzzled over her overanxious manner.

One day, the pastor was surprised to see Marianne's husband at his office. The husband asked if he might speak to the pastor about his wife. He explained that he was concerned and frustrated with his wife's behavior. She was constantly working on this church project, making lists and more lists, but didn't seem to get anywhere. In addition, she would check the lists so much before going out to church or to work that they would be constantly late for activities. He admitted that his wife had always been a "checker" and a "worrier," repeatedly checking the stove and the locks on the doors. Sometimes the husband could distract her from repeatedly doing this, but now he was quite exasperated with her. The new obsession over the church project was the last straw. She was constantly talking to him about the plans until he was sick of it. She would call everybody on the committee and repeat her concerns to the point where her husband felt she might be alienating the members. But his biggest complaint was that she spent so much time checking and praying over her lists that nothing else was being done in the house. He really felt bad about all this because he could see when he confronted his wife that she was very sorry, but she did not know how to stop. She seemed compelled to do all this and when she tried to stop and attend to other matters, she became even more anxious. She was now constantly late for work, church, and all social activities. The pastor consoled the husband and offered to speak to Marianne. After praying together, the husband thanked the pastor for his help.

The next Sunday, the pastor approached Marianne and explained what he had learned from her husband. Marianne at first looked very troubled but then with a sigh of relief and resignation admitted, "I know this is ridiculous, and I know I have to break out of this, but I am just at a loss." She then turned toward him and in a desperate and defeated manner asked, "Pastor, can you help me?"

DISCUSSION

How does one reply to this plea for help? If one is not acquainted with Marianne's condition, it will be difficult to know what to say. Some hunt for spiritual explanations for this malady. Others offer speculations based on their understanding of emotional issues. In the area of pastoral counseling, the clergyperson is often expected to have an explanation for all that befalls humankind. However, proverbial wisdom teaches, "An honest answer is like a kiss on the lips."[1] Sometimes the humility expressed in the admission, "I don't know much about what you are going through, but I will try to help you get the answers," paves the road for successful pastoral intervention.

Obsessive-compulsive disorder, the diagnosis for Marianne's condition, was once thought to be uncommon. Recently, studies have shown that it is relatively frequent, occurring in about

2.5 percent of the population.[2] This disorder is often unrecognized, and sufferers tend to keep their problems secret. The hallmarks of this condition are the presence of obsessions and/or compulsions. Obsessions are repetitive, intrusive thoughts, impulses, or images that repeatedly plague a person's mind. These obsessions are experienced as distressing and inappropriate. Adults with OCD will recognize that these obsessions are excessive and unrealistic. Children with OCD may not be able to make such a determination and thus believe their obsessive thoughts.

Compulsions are defined as repeated behaviors that attempt to quell the anxiety generated by the obsessions. For example, a person such as Marianne may have performed the repetitive checking behaviors in response to some intrusive obsession such as "If I don't check my lists, the stove, or the locks, something terrible will happen." Marianne recognizes that this is an unrealistic and irrational thought, but she will find that it will continue to recur and cause her to be a slave to her compulsive checking.

People with obsessive-compulsive disorder (OCD) will find that this disease causes a major disturbance in the ability to function in their occupational life as well as in their daily routine. They may find that these repetitive thoughts and acts are time consuming. These behaviors can consume hours of time each day and progress to the point where one cannot function normally. Often, the degree of stress on mental life can cause significant problems with a person's ability to concentrate on academic or job responsibilities and may affect the person's relationships. In the worst-case scenario, a person can be virtually housebound, as in the case of Marianne. She spends all her time with her obsessions and compulsions, which render her unable to perform her job, participate in her church ministry, or even take care of her home or personal hygiene. In many patients, OCD can lead to a clinical depression.

A variety of obsessions and compulsions can affect a person's life. The most common obsessions include a fear of contamination, a fear that one has left something undone, pathological doubt about oneself or a situation involving oneself. Upsetting sexual thoughts or images, intrusive thoughts of violence, or excessive worry that one has inadvertently hurt another are also frequent. Inexplicable anxiety may occur for some if objects are not in a certain order, whether it be symmetrically or numerically determined.

Many forms of obsessions are idiosyncratic and individualistic. No matter how unusual the obsessions or compulsions, all cause distress and anxiety and are recognized as being intrusive and inappropriate by the OCD sufferer. Repetitive compulsions, whether behaviors or repeated mental activities, are performed to quell the anxiety generated by the obsession. These would include compulsions to repeatedly wash one's hands if one has a marked fear of contamination or repeated checking rituals.

As with obsessions, compulsions can take on many different forms in different individuals. In Marianne's case, she had a repeated need to check her lists to look for things that she felt she might have left undone. She also checked her stove and locks constantly, not being satisfied that she had already checked. Other compulsive behaviors include counting rituals, hoarding, or compulsive hair pulling (trichotillomania).

These manifestations of OCD are common to non-Christians, as well. However, a number of compulsions may not be recognized as such because they appear to fit the perceived norms of the Christian life. An example of this is compulsive praying in response to an obsession. Although Christians recognize that praying is an important part of spiritual life, compulsive praying is excessive, prolonged, and despite its time consumption does not quell the anxiety caused by the obsession. After treatment, many Christians recognize the difference between genuine, faithful praying, and obsessional praying.

Other manifestations of OCD among Christians may include pathologic doubt regarding one's salvation or doubt about one's ability to be forgiven. This is called "scrupulosity," which entails having a false sense of guilt and a perception that one has done something wrong, but there is no evidence for it. It can include doubts regarding one's spiritual life. One can imagine the complexities involved in discerning between acceptance of the doctrine of the sinful nature of humans versus the manifestations of scrupulosity in OCD.

One point of distinction is that Christians with OCD will find it difficult to draw the expected comfort from scriptural promises if they are in opposition to their obsessive worry. For example, individuals who have pathological doubt regarding their personal salvation would have trouble believing, as they once did, the personal application of John 3:16, "For God so loved the world that he gave his one and only Son, that whoever believes in him shall not perish but have eternal life."[3] They often question themselves regarding their Christian status. And despite repeated recitation of scriptural promises by loved ones, they remain doubtful about truths such as 1 John 1:9, "If we confess our sins, he is faithful and just and will forgive us our sins and purify us from all unrighteousness."[4] This pathologic doubt robs Christians of peace and joy, and may interfere with ministries that they had been quite capable of performing when they were not afflicted. Almost any aspect of religious life can be incorporated into the obsessions and compulsions. Therefore, it is important for Christians to recognize OCD in themselves or a family member. Dr. Bruce Ballard of Cornell University Medical College states, "Activities that seem so deviant from the norm of those who are intensely religious are clues to the possibility of underlying emotional disturbance. This is the model one uses to ascertain whether certain behaviors fit within a person's cultural background or would be viewed as abnormal by others within the culture."[5]

Many cases go unrecognized because the obsessions are often kept secret and the compulsions are often not done in public. As a result, the individual may withdraw from peers, consumed by the obsessions and compulsions, leaving most to wonder what happened. Even in Marianne's case, family members may not fully understand the psychological processes that cause this disturbing condition. Nevertheless, individuals suffer a great deal of anguish when they experience obsessions and compulsions. This is made worse because they recognize that their thoughts are inappropriate. Intensely embarrassed and ashamed of their thoughts, they suffer in silence.

Many patients with OCD demonstrate a waxing and waning course during their lifetimes with periods of exacerbation, which can occur spontaneously or under times of stress. A small percentage develop a downhill course in their ability to function at work or socially.

In the past decade, many advances have been made in the treatment of obsessive-compulsive disorder. Effective medications include Anafranil, Prozac, Luvox, Zoloft, and Paxil. These drugs work to regulate a chemical in the brain called serotonin, which goes awry in OCD. Once the medication is started, it may be several weeks before some improvement is noticed. When it happens, many patients report that the intrusiveness of the thoughts diminish or become less distressing. Psychological treatments are designed to assist the patient in controlling compulsions and coping with obsessions. A person with OCD needs to learn various ways of halting intrusive thoughts, e.g., "thought stopping." Some find that snapping a rubber band on the wrist when experiencing the intrusive thoughts may help prevent the obsession from taking hold. Others try to visualize a big "STOP" sign. Still others may find distraction helps to escape the obsession.

It is important that sufferers seek treatment from professionals to learn important coping tools that work best for them. Compulsions that result from obsessive thoughts such as checking behaviors can also be approached. Generally, curbing compulsions can be practiced by continually exposing oneself to situations that may promote obsessive thinking and then preventing oneself from giving in to the compulsion. Eventually, toleration of the anxiety occurs by not performing the compulsion and the anxiety decreases with time and practice. These techniques result in less time spent on compulsive behaviors and improved ability to function. Public awareness has increased concerning the frequency of obsessive-compulsive disorder and its diagnosis. Because effective treatments are available, people such as Marianne have the potential to obtain relief from symptoms. Education and emotional support are needed to help sufferers realize that their obsessions are unrealistic and that they can develop the means to resume their lives and ministries.

A psychiatric evaluation for OCD is a good way to obtain necessary treatment. What should one expect in a psychiatric evaluation? This is generally done as an interview in which a patient's symptoms are identified as the chief complaint. Further clarification of these symptoms is obtained including duration, how much one's functions are limited, the nature of the obsessions and compulsions, recent stressors, and whether anything the patient has tried has been helpful. The psychiatrist will then ask for pertinent medical history such as whether this has occurred before and whether any particular treatments have been tried. Questions about emotional or relationship difficulties are often asked in an attempt to identify coexisting conditions or to make a more accurate alternative diagnoses. A patient's medical history including illnesses, results of recent physical evaluation, medications taken, relevant blood and laboratory tests is also important information to provide. Other questions involving interpersonal relationships, drug or substance abuse, and family history of psychiatric disorders are also asked.

The psychiatrist then performs a mental status examination, which is composed of observations and questions directed at evaluating many areas of mental functioning. These include appearance, speech, mood, and cognitive abilities such as memory and concentration. Judgment and insight into the illness are also determined. Questions about suicidal, homicidal, or delusional thinking are also part of a thorough mental status examination. Given the extensive and probing questions that are explored in a psychiatric evaluation, a word must be said about confidentiality. Professional ethics as well as the common law uphold the privacy and confidentiality of all information provided by a client, patient, penitent, etc., to the respective professional, whether it be therapist, physician, clergyman, or attorney. Hence, unless a person gives permission, generally in written form, information divulged in psychiatric evaluations must be kept confidential.

Discerning the difference between theological and psychological issues will lead to proper assessment of a person's difficulty. Ministers can play an important role in helping individuals afflicted with mental health problems. Christians with OCD, particularly those who suffer from excessive doubt or scrupulosity, are often anxious about their spiritual condition. They tend to focus more on God's judgment and wrath rather than on His grace. Because OCD is an anxiety disorder, sufferers tend to glean from Scripture those verses that cause them to worry about their spiritual well-being, while taking only transient comfort from Scripture pertaining to God's love and forgiveness.

Ministers probably have experienced this with some members of their congregations who just cannot take comfort from the reassurances of their counsel or the promises of God. Hence ministers, educated about OCD, can best identify those persons whose spiritual questioning may be a symptom of OCD or just the normal concerns of a growing believer. The differences are often subtle and elusive but are worthy of deliberation.

HOW CHRISTIANS CAN HELP

The following are ways in which a caring Christian, whether it be a fellow churchgoer, family member, or the minister, can help.

If a person is suffering from a mental problem, make attempts to learn more about it instead of making immediate speculations or spiritual judgments about his or her condition. Many places provide information about OCD. One such place is the Obsessive-Compulsive Disorder Foundation, Inc., located in Milford, Connecticut. When you contact the foundation, you will receive an information packet that contains:

   a. A list of books and educational materials on OCD
   b. Brochure titled, *Giving Obsessive-Compulsives Another Lifestyle (G.O.A.L.)*
   c. Brochure titled, *How to Select a Behavior Therapist*
   d. Brochure titled, *Obsessive-Compulsive Disorder in School-Age Children*
   e. A current edition of the OCD Foundation newsletter
   f. A list of professionals who treat OCD as well as support groups in your local area.

The OCD Foundation also has a Web site that has links to other information sites as well. In addition, the foundation sponsors conferences throughout the country designed specifically for those who are afflicted with OCD and is a valuable source of current information in the field.

Maintain a stance of steady encouragement. Use Scripture, but be aware that the individual will require continual reassurance and patience. It can be very frustrating trying to reassure someone who has OCD or "the doubting disease." However, if you keep in mind that the doubt and anxiety represent symptoms of an illness much like a cough is a symptom of pneumonia, then you can avoid the temptation to believe that your attempts to reassure are being ignored. Instead, recall the person's usual manner of thinking prior to the development of OCD, or what we call the baseline state, as being truly representative of the individual.

Relationships can be stressed by an individual's bout with OCD. As a caring person, try not to take the sufferer's idiosyncratic thoughts personally. For example, one who has contamination fears may not enter your home or touch specific items that belong to you. Do not defend your personal cleanliness or insist that he or she enter your domain. However, maintain an open invitation because the individual may be able to venture out and expose himself or herself to fears when ready. This usually occurs in the context of treatment in which patients are taught coping skills and encouraged to practice exposing themselves to the object of their obsessive anxiety.

How can the minister or the caring individual tell when someone might have OCD and be in need of professional help? If someone reveals that he or she is troubled by thoughts and behaviors that are described in this chapter, provide the person with an opportunity to tell you more about these symptoms. Try to ascertain the level of distress this is causing the individual and his or her family. Generally, most people are quite secretive about their condition, functioning quite well despite troubling thoughts. Usually when they confide in others, their level of distress is fairly significant and the chances are good that they would benefit from professional help.

A sure sign that professional attention is necessary occurs when a decline occurs in the person's ability to function at work, school, or home. Obsessive thoughts and compulsive behaviors may be so time consuming that they prevent a person from attending to the tasks of daily living or even something as simple as getting out of the house on time. A decline may occur in the person's usual level of service or participation in the church. Activities that were once performed enthusiastically may turn into obstacles and burdens. When questioned, the sufferer may complain that he or she would like to be a faithful servant but just feels so overwhelmed. This is a good opening to provide a safe, nonjudgmental opportunity to discuss the person's worries.

If you discover that the individual may be suffering from OCD and it is clear that functioning has been affected, professional help should be recommended. The caring individual can point out to the sufferer that treatment will preserve or restore functioning at work, home, and church. It would also address emotional suffering and have a positive impact on his or her spiritual health.

A crucial factor warranting a prompt referral to professional help is the presence of a clinical depression. A higher risk of developing a depression exists in people who have obsessive-compulsive disorder. This can occur simultaneously or at different times in a person's life. The description of a clinical depression is presented in Chapter 7. Suffice it to say that the presence of depression should be a signal to make a timely referral for professional help.

Help the individual combat the stigma often attached to seeking mental health services. Unfortunately, a stigma in society regarding mental illness has crossed into many churches. Hence, sufferers with OCD symptoms are reluctant to admit their thoughts and behaviors and even much more disinclined to seek professional attention. Wise counsel from the caring individual is needed. For example, stress that taking care of one's mental health is akin to taking care of oneself physically and represents good stewardship of our bodies.

Reassure the person that you would not think less of him or her for seeking help but rather offer congratulations for showing courage. If you are acquainted with any similar situations, present to the person instances in which someone has benefited from professional help. Try to do this without providing any identifying detail about another person, as many individuals value their privacy on this sensitive topic.

Shed light on the unknown. Describe what takes place in a psychiatric examination as outlined earlier in this chapter. Share information you have obtained on the topic of OCD and how one finds professional help. If you need assistance on the latter, refer to the listing of resources at the end of this chapter.

Assist the family members. Because OCD impairs the functioning of the sufferer, it is important to pay attention to the needs of the family and the household. As you can imagine, OCD can cause much time loss because of the mental and behavioral rituals that consume the sufferer. Job functioning may be impaired, leading to a loss of income. Household chores may be left undone. A caring community can do a great deal to meet the specific needs of the family members until the sufferer regains his or her mental health. The time this requires is variable and help may be necessary from weeks to months. Generally speaking, many people who suffer from OCD function despite their illness and can be restored to good functioning in a timely way with professional help and support from their friends and families.

Respect the individual's confidentiality. This dictum is self-explanatory. However, there may be many areas in the course of church life in which a person's desire for privacy may be violated inadvertently. For example, if a person requests prayer for the problem, it may have to be done tactfully without telling the details to those who are praying or limited to the confines of a minister's office. One should ask permission of the sufferer should there be any reason to discuss the matter with others in the family or in the church. Many people with OCD choose to conceal their condition even when they are improving with treatment. They may be doing so for personal and valid reasons, and it would be important for the clergy and the caring individual to honor their wishes.

Assist the individual in getting professional help. Getting the appropriate help for the person with OCD may require some planning and research. In general, the treatment for OCD in this country involves a type of behavior therapy, oftentimes in conjunction with medication. Psychologists, social workers, and Christian counselors who have specific expertise in the cognitive-behavioral or behavioral treatment of obsessive-compulsive disorder are equipped to provide the talking aspect of the therapy. However, they cannot dispense medication and would have to make a referral to a psychiatrist for an appropriate medication evaluation. Sometimes, although this is not the optimal situation, such patients may go to their family doctor for medication.

A psychiatrist is a medical doctor who can perform a psychiatric evaluation and prescribe medication appropriately. The majority of psychiatrists provide psychotherapy in conjunction with medication as needed and it would be advisable to see a psychiatrist with expertise in the treatment of anxiety disorders such as OCD. Some hospitals in the local community may operate anxiety disorder programs that provide multidisciplinary services for patients. They may be staffed by a combination of psychologists, social workers, counselors, and psychiatrists who offer a comprehensive treatment program. You may wish to contact your local hospital's department of psychiatry to ascertain whether or not such a program exists either at the hospital or in a community mental health clinic.

You can further inquire if there is a private psychiatrist affiliated with the hospital or in the community who has expertise in treating OCD. Your family physician may also be a source of information in providing you with a referral to a psychiatrist or therapist he or she regards and believes will benefit the patient. After trying your local resources for referrals, you may wish to contact the following national organizations.

RESOURCES

Obsessive-Compulsive Disorder Foundation, Inc.
9 Depot Street
Milford, CT 06460
(203) 878-5669
www.ocfoundation.org

This organization provides referrals to practitioners whether they be psychiatrists or therapists throughout the nation specializing in the treatment of OCD. They can assist you with names, addresses, and telephone numbers in your specific region. When requesting a referral, you should ask for an information packet that contains helpful information described previously.

* * *

American Psychiatric Association
Division of Public Affairs
Department MM99
1400 K Street NW
Washington, DC 20005
(888) 357-7924

This is the professional organization for psychiatrists in this country. It has a large membership divided into district branches across the nation. To obtain a referral in your area, you need to contact your local branch of the APA. You can get this information by calling the APA Answer Center at the toll-free number, (888) 35-PSYCH. Once you obtain the number of your local branch, you can obtain referrals to private psychiatrists in or near your area. Information about the psychiatrists are kept in a database and are available upon request. Ask for someone whose expertise is in treating OCD or anxiety disorders, in addition to any other specific needs you may have. This can include accessibility, language spoken, or individual issues that concern you.

* * *

New Life Clinics
820 West Spring Creek Parkway
Plano, TX 75115
(800) NEW-LIFE

The New Life Clinics represent a series of mental health facilities throughout the United States that has a distinctly Christian perspective. When you call the above telephone number, you can obtain referrals to either New Life Clinics in your locale or a referral to a Christian therapist or psychiatrist from their registry. A trained Christian counselor will take your information and questions and make a suitable referral if it exists in their listings. It is important to ask for someone with expertise in treating OCD, and if possible, someone capable of dispensing medication if needed.

* * *

Focus on the Family Program
Colorado Springs, CO 80995
(719) 531-3400 Ext. 2700

This Christian program provides a nationwide registry of Christian professionals whom they have screened through an application process. When you call this number, a trained counselor in the Counseling Department will speak to you and make an appropriate referral from their registry. When you speak to the counselor, provide some details about your problem and ask for a referral to someone with expertise in treating OCD or anxiety disorders. For ministers, they also have a "Pastoral Care and Education Department" that may assist ministers with informative programs. This program's telephone number is (719) 531-3400.

Chapter 2

Panic: The "Oppressor"

Kim, a young pastor trained in Korea, was invited to come to the United States to continue his work among the churches in a large city. A gifted speaker, he was extremely dedicated to his work, preparing for his sermons in a methodical and thorough manner. He was well received by the churches that he visited, and people often looked forward to the times when he would deliver the message. Kim was delighted about his successful speaking engagements in the United States despite the fact that at times he was anxious about different aspects of life in his new environment.

During the winter of his first year in this country, he began to experience a strange sense of foreboding. Each time as he was preparing for a sermon, he became intensely anxious and at times felt that he was paralyzed and unable to function. Quite often, out of the blue, he would experience episodes of intense anxiety, sweating, and feelings of impending doom as his heart pounded furiously. He attributed these attacks to "spiritual oppression" as he felt that these attacks were designed to impede his work in preaching. He found comfort in prayer and meditation and continued to persevere in his work. He shared some of his problems with senior pastors in various churches, and they all acknowledged that the work of the ministry can be at times stressful and met with opposition. They all shared their experiences with Kim and encouraged him and prayed for him. He did derive a sense of comfort from these meetings.

His symptoms began to worsen throughout that winter and even into the early spring. These attacks became frequent and occurred regularly as often as three times a day. They were sudden and came out of the blue, but at times Kim did notice that they would be triggered by his preparation for a sermon. He called this thing the "monster." He fought furiously to ignore the symptoms and remain calm, in order to persevere with his work. He decided that a visit to the doctor might be helpful so he made an appointment with a local internist. He was reassured that his entire physical exam was normal, and he was proclaimed to be in a "good state of health."

The "monster" continued to afflict Kim. He longed to return to his homeland and get some rest. His mental turmoil and grueling schedule had been very draining. How he longed to truly rest. His mind, which was at the height of unrest, began to dwell on these recurrent attacks and whether or not he would be able to function as a minister. He lived in fear of the "monster's" approach and presence. True, he could distract himself by prayer, taking long walks, and getting involved with the people in his church. However, the distractions did not last very long and soon he began worrying again. He found himself avoiding people and places where he would not be able to escape, should the "monster" reappear. The worry began to turn into despair. Finally, one spring day he sat down at his desk to write his letter of resignation to his pastor.

Dear Reverend,

I know that in the work of the Lord there is persecution and opposition from the enemy, and alas, I think that my troubles have been from such a cause. But I find that I am in such a weakened state that my faith, which I thought had no bounds, is really minuscule in size. I find that it does not sustain me to do the work that I've been called to do; therefore, I am most saddened by having to write this letter of resignation.

It seems that this thing that I call the "monster" leaves me intensely fearful and shaken and has affected my ability to work. It haunts me daily. It causes me to avoid the very people who I long to serve. I could no longer in good conscience preach from the pulpit toward a goal of strengthening the congregation when I now cower in fear when alone in my room. My hope is to return to Korea and from that point I do not know what the future holds. I am sorry to do this because I really don't wish to leave this work that I wished my whole life to do. Under the circumstances I find that there is no other recourse.

Respectfully,
Kim

When the senior pastor read this letter, he closed his eyes and began to reflect on Kim's ministry in the United States. What a shame that this gifted young man would have to abandon his work because of this affliction. And what was this affliction? The senior pastor, who was unused to not having answers, began to ponder. Is this a spiritual oppression of the "enemy?" Is this the manifestation of an overly stressed mind? Could these be the symptoms of a yet undiagnosed medical illness? He felt quite helpless at discovering the explanation. But he was convinced that an answer must be obtained and that Kim should not have to give up his brilliant work because of this undefined, inexplicable problem. "What should I do?" he asked himself.

DISCUSSION

Kim is suffering from a classic case of panic disorder. Panic attacks are episodes of intense anxiety that often develop "out of the blue." They are characterized by physical symptoms such as sweating, heart palpitations, flushing, "a sensation of knots in the stomach," shakiness, dizziness, and other symptoms that often accompany anxiety. In addition, when one is undergoing a panic attack one's thoughts usually resemble the following: "Something terrible is going to happen to me" or "I am losing my mind." These are called thoughts of impending doom. Often, people attribute these symptoms to a physical condition. As a result they may make frequent trips to the doctor or the hospital emergency room only to learn each time that they have a clean bill of health.

Many problems may result from panic attacks. When the attacks reach a certain frequency or cause significant anticipation of future attacks, we call this condition panic disorder. People often live in fear of having a panic attack once they experience their first one. If a person begins to avoid situations that might trigger such an attack or avoid places where he or she cannot flee should a panic attack occur, a condition has developed known as agoraphobia. The degree of agoraphobia may vary. Some people persevere and function despite multiple panic attacks and will try not to avoid places or activities but will experience distress during these times. On the other side of the spectrum, some people become so agoraphobic that they are virtually housebound.

Many people refer to the panic attack as "the monster" because of its suddenness, intensity, and unpredictability. They truly feel as if they are plagued by a monster. Patients have described panic attacks as "a monkey on my back," "a green monster waiting to pounce" or a "shadowy figure lurking behind." Others insist that it is a hidden, undiagnosed medical problem that cannot be psychological. They spend a great deal of time at emergency rooms and many doctors' offices getting multiple second opinions.

Among Christians, another common conceptualization of the panic attack is that it represents "spiritual oppression," in other words, that the causative agent is a demon oppressor. In Kim's case, having found no medical reason for his attacks and not recognizing this problem as that of an anxiety disorder, his conclusion was that it represented "spiritual attack from the enemy."

This formulation was not accurate in Kim's case. Recognizing that this was a classic case of panic disorder might have led him to seek appropriate treatment. According to Dr. Jerrold Rosenbaum of the Department of Psychiatry at Harvard Medical School, "the key to effective treatment of panic disorder is early recognition of the condition. . . . Early referral to a psychiatrist or a psychologist can be cost effective in the long run."[1]

Detection and treatment would not only relieve the anxiety symptoms, but would have allowed Kim to stay and continue the important work that he was doing in the United States. In addition, he might have had a different perspective on his faith, which he branded to be poor in his resignation letter.

There are effective treatments for panic disorder and agoraphobia. These would include psychological therapies such as cognitive-behavioral therapy designed for individuals and groups who suffer from panic disorder. Cognitive-behavioral therapy is a form of "talking therapy" in which certain automatic, anxiety-provoking thoughts are identified and corrected. For example, if a rodlike structure is held to your head and you believe it to be a gun, then you will be highly anxious. On the other hand, if you believe it to be a pen, then you will remain calm. Hence, people's perception of a given situation governs their mood. If they have learned to automatically give the most negative attribution to every situation, they will no doubt be constantly anxious.

Often these thoughts are irrational, unrealistic, and catastrophic, and in the case of the Christian believer, they are usually not biblical. It is therefore important in therapy to unlearn old patterns of thinking and learn to restructure one's appraisal of reality. Automatic, catastrophic thoughts are contradicted by Scripture such as Jeremiah 29:11, "For I know the plans I have for you," declares the Lord, "plans to prosper you and not to harm you, plans to give you hope and a future."[2] In therapy the Christian can learn to use individualized, biblically based as well as other realistic, positive thoughts to replace anxiety-provoking ones.

Relaxation techniques are used to relieve the physical tension produced in panic disorder. During relaxation, the person is asked to focus on and relax muscle groups in a systematic way. For example, one may start by relaxing the hand and arm muscles, followed by the facial, chest, abdominal, and leg muscles. The individual may be asked to visualize a relaxing scene, such as a sandy beach on a beautiful day. By practicing these techniques daily, the person learns how to gain control over the body and decrease physical tension.

The other aspect of cognitive-behavioral therapy addresses agoraphobia. People suffering from panic disorder may begin to develop avoidance behaviors, such as refraining from entering public places or from traveling beyond a "safety zone" for fear of having a panic attack. This condition, called agoraphobia, may culminate in the worst-case scenario in which a person is housebound. It takes a good deal of personal motivation to overcome agoraphobia. These individuals must take gradual steps to expose themselves to traveling outside the home. Such steps will produce some anxiety that must be tolerated. Persistence will eventually lead to venturing out with more ease, a process called habituation. Homework assignments are designed in therapy to practice exposure to feared places according to an individualized hierarchy. Avoidance behaviors are discouraged as they lead to further restrictions and limitations in function. As the person ventures into feared places and keeps a consistent pattern of doing so, he or she will gradually be less anxious. Unrealistic, catastrophic thoughts can be replaced with more calming ones. For example, "There is no evidence that going into this restaurant has the power to cause a panic attack," versus "What if I have a panic attack at this restaurant?" The "what if . . ." statements frequently plague the thinking of anxious people. Often the "what if . . ." represents the worst possible scenario. In addition, the likelihood of it occurring is exceedingly low but is highly overestimated in the mind of the anxious person. Managing the "what ifs . . ." with objectivity and discarding them as highly unlikely is a practical help to the sufferer.

Many people with panic disorder misinterpret normal bodily sensations as abnormal and as a sign of a medical emergency. Sensations such as a rapid heart rate in response to heat, anger, excitement, or exercise are mistakenly perceived as a sign of a heart problem or the beginnings of a panic attack. This misinterpretation alone will generate sufficient anxiety to fuel a panic attack. Stopping the vicious cycle at the very beginning by saying to oneself that the heart normally beats faster under certain conditions and that this response is characteristic of a well-functioning cardiac system will thwart the rise in anxiety. For some reason, anxious people are more keenly sensitive to bodily sensations while most people are not even aware of them. Therefore, they need to learn that they tend to misinterpret these sensations, and correcting such misinterpretations of health threats will be extremely helpful.

Thankfully, a host of medications have been found to be effective in ameliorating the symptoms of panic. Such medications include high potency tranquilizers such as Xanax (alprazolam) and Klonopin (clonazepam). A variety of antidepressants have also been found effective in treating panic disorder. They include Tofranil (imipramine), Pamelor (desipramine), and the newer medications such as Prozac (fluoxetine) and Zoloft (sertraline).

Many people who complain of panic attacks may actually suffer from depression as well. Hence, treating these patients with antidepressants is indicated. Proper psychiatric evaluations of people suffering from panic disorder would determine the appropriate medication. Treatment may involve psychotherapy alone or a combination of psychotherapy and medication. It is worth mentioning that medical conditions mimicking panic disorder should be considered and ruled out. Common conditions mimicking panic disorder include thyroid disease, cardiac problems such as arrhythmias or mitral valve prolapse, tumors of the adrenal gland, and many others. Drug and alcohol abuse or withdrawal, excessive use of caffeine, or certain over-the-counter medications can produce panic-like symptoms. A good psychiatric evaluation would be able to distinguish these factors.

Kim's life might have changed with early recognition and intervention. Not only would early intervention have made an impact on his life, but also for those around him. Because this form of anxiety can lead to demoralization and depression, one needs to seek help as soon as possible. Panic disorder may have a familial predisposition. Certainly, looking at family history might be helpful in identifying other members who may be similarly afflicted. Again, early recognition, proper education, and treatment may improve the quality of life, function, and ministries of all who suffer from panic disorder.

HOW CHRISTIANS CAN HELP

There are a number of ways Christians can help those who suffer from panic disorder and agoraphobia. The following suggestions include some pragmatic as well as theoretical considerations. Some are geared for the clergyman while other suggestions have a wider application to include all caring individuals.

A minister or caring individual must always consider all the health components of those under his or her care. Naturally, spiritual health is the expertise of the trained clergy, but in the situation of anxiety symptoms and particularly in panic disorder, it is crucial not to forget the physical health of the individual. This is because the anxiety may be a symptom of a hidden physical or medical condition that must be detected in order to properly help the person. Therefore, the minister should inquire about the person's physical health and whether he or she has consulted a physician.

If medical attention has not been sought for the panic attacks, the minister can urge the person to do so. This simple suggestion is often gratefully received by the sufferer. There are at least two explanations for this. First, it reduces anxiety by providing a possible medical explanation to the sufferer who has been gripped by many unanswered questions about the oppressive panic attacks. Second, the referral to a physician for a complete medical examination offers the sufferer the comfort of knowing all avenues of investigation are being explored to find an answer to the problem. It demonstrates to the sufferer that the clergyperson is interested in his or her total health and is not quick to couch everything in a spiritual framework. When ministers make such a recommendation to their congregant, it provides a sense of assurance to the individual that the person's total condition—biological as well as spiritual needs—is being addressed. Most individuals who come for psychiatric evaluation are reassured when their medical status is investigated. A minister can play a vital role in initiating this process by suggesting it to the sufferer of panic attacks.

Once the medical evaluation is done by the internist or the family doctor, two outcomes are possible. One is that the doctor has identified a medical illness causing panic attacks, and begins the appropriate treatment. The other, which is quite common, is that the sufferer receives a clean bill of health. The doctor may make a referral to a mental health professional, be it a psychiatrist, psychologist, or therapist. A caring Christian should support and assist the sufferer in following up on the referral. The sufferer may have many issues that make it difficult for him or her to obtain mental health care. Many of these issues relate to false ideas about having a mental problem and the stigma that is prevalent in society and even in the church. Going for mental health care may represent a substantial blow to self-esteem. A caring individual can be very helpful to the sufferer by showing support for this action and framing it in a positive way.

The minister or the caring individual may need to assist the sufferer in getting the appropriate mental health care, particularly if the person continues to suffer acutely from the panic attacks. The majority of people with panic disorder in this country benefit from either cognitive-behavioral psychotherapy, medications, or in most cases a combination of both. Hence, one should try to find treatment in resources that provide both modalities of treatment, such as a psychiatrist with expertise in the cognitive-behavioral treatment of panic disorder, a therapist who works closely with a psychiatrist dispensing medications, or anxiety disorder programs who staff a team that provides the different modalities of treatment. The reader can also utilize the resources provided at the end of Chapter 1.

The Anxiety Disorders Association of America can be a source of valuable information. The association provides a national listing of professionals who have expertise in the area of panic disorder and other anxiety disorders. A general information packet about the organization as well as literature on a particular anxiety disorder can be requested. In addition, the organization publishes a catalog of excellent books that can be purchased. Self-help and relaxation tapes are also sold. Relaxation tapes are designed to train the listener to relax mind and body using various techniques introduced on the tape. This may involve corrective breathing, muscle relaxation, and visual imagery. Many variations of such tapes are available in the secular arena. The Anxiety Disorders Association of America also publishes a quarterly newsletter for members that highlights progress in the field of anxiety which is of interest to consumers and professionals. Their address and telephone number are listed in the resource section of this chapter.

The caring individual or minister is advised to learn as much as he or she can about panic disorder. Having a clear understanding about the illness would give one a sense of the severity of the attacks and how frightening and incapacitating they can be. Psychoeducation, which is the education of the patient, the family members, or other involved individuals has been an important element of the therapy of panic disorder. Hence, ministers can participate in such a process as they care for their afflicted member.

One area that warrants further understanding is the topic of risk versus benefit when it comes to the use of medication in treating panic disorder. When medications are considered in treatment, the psychiatrist or medical doctor will discuss the pros and cons of a particular drug and what is expected from its use. Each of the different classes of drugs in the treatment of panic disorder has its own benefits and side effects. Make sure the doctor outlines them for you. Perhaps the physician may provide literature summarizing these points. After this is done, a discussion ensues in which the patient deliberates the benefits versus potential risks and makes a decision as to whether he or she wants to take the medication. Having been reasonably informed and discussing all options with the doctor including what is to be expected if no medication is taken, the patient then decides whether he or she wants to take the drug. This discussion is essential for a complete psychiatric consultation. Although this interchange results from the collaborative thinking of the patient and doctor, the final decision reflects the thinking of the patient who has considered many variables to make a decision that is best for his or her life at the current time.

Caring individuals can learn a great deal by listening and supporting the sufferer's decision-making process. They should never make generalized statements about medications, even if there are side effects. Most medications do have some side effects, but they may improve over time. Instead, try to understand what the sufferer is willing to tolerate in light of the clear benefits of the medication utilized. Serious negative side effects and risks should have been discussed by the doctor with the patient. The patient should be careful to monitor for such serious consequences or side effects. If this were to occur, then the patient should be encouraged to contact his or her doctor immediately, and the medication may have to be stopped.

Many patients who suffer from panic disorder benefit from books written on the subject. These are generally written by those who have personally experienced the illness and the process of treatment. Some are written by experts in the field directed toward a general audience. Contact the Anxiety Disorders Association of America for a catalog of books and tapes.

Be a good coach in the fight against agoraphobia. Agoraphobia, or avoidance behavior, commonly complicates the life of the individual suffering from panic attacks. In an attempt to avoid triggering panic attacks, he or she avoids places where panic attacks have occurred or where there is no easy means of escape without being noticed or possibly embarrassed. How can the caring Christian help? It is very important that the caring individual does not worsen the situation by being an "enabler" of the avoidant behavior. Avoidance can lead to a restricted lifestyle with the most tragic situation of being housebound and not functioning. Caring individuals may unwittingly participate in such a process and thus enable the agoraphobic to lead a more and more restricted lifestyle. Misguided by strong feelings of sympathy for the sufferer, caring individuals can inadvertently make it easier for the individual to restrict activities and thus "enable" him or her to avoid.

The goal of treatment is the exact opposite. Through a process of talk therapy and homework, the patient is asked to increase exposure to the outside and especially to feared places. Hence, a caring individual must be aware of his or her own contribution to this process whether it be by enabling regressive, avoidant behavior that may feel more comfortable to the patient or whether it is the more positive role of encouraging the patient to move forward even though it is anxiety provoking.

For example, suppose a person is afraid to return to work because the first panic attack occurred while on the train going to work. This person wants to avoid traveling on the train because of the belief that another panic attack will occur while riding on the train. An "enabler" would agree with the person's presumption and would support the notion that he or she should not go to work in order to avoid panic attacks. This is counterproductive and fosters agoraphobia. On the other hand, the caring individual would do well to coax the person to make attempts to get back on the train or simply reinforce the idea that getting back on the train is an important goal. Naturally, this is more easily said than done since panic disorder can cause a great deal of anticipatory anxiety in the person contemplating getting back on the train. When resistance or a great deal of difficulty is present, professional help can provide the means and coping skills to achieve this goal.

Caring individuals have to negotiate a balance between not being too sympathetic and thus enabling avoidance versus being too harsh and critical in expecting the sufferer to surmount fears quickly. This process requires time and professional help. Perhaps the best conceptualization for the role of the caring individual, whether it be the minister or a family member, is that of a good "coach." The coach congratulates the individual when he or she is willing to venture out and make progress despite significant anxiety, but does not demoralize or criticize when a person succumbs to fears. Such a stance would be most supportive to the sufferer. This is especially important while he or she is in treatment as it can augment the work done in therapy.

To conclude this chapter on panic disorder and how Christians can help, it is worthwhile to underscore some aspects of the integration of theology and psychology. While these can remain separate universes of discourse for most people, integration of the two areas may provide a great benefit for the clergyperson trying to help the congregant. It is unfortunate that proponents in each of these areas view each other with suspicion and at times overt hostility. Where possible, a minister should have a conceptual framework that embodies the truth from religious beliefs integrated with models of psychological concepts. This can be most beneficial to the person suffering from anxiety.

To illustrate, let us look at the concept of fear. The Christian community has understood at least two sides to fear. There is the good fear embodied in the notion of "the fear of the Lord" which embraces the belief that Christians should have a genuine, reverential trust in God in order to negotiate life wisely and successfully. Biblical support for this can be found in Psalm 115:11, "Ye that fear the Lord, trust in the Lord: He is their help and their shield."[3] This is contrasted with a negative side of fear which describes a fearful and timid spirit that prevents a Christian from doing what God wants from him or her. This is evident in Moses' fear of leading his people out of Egypt when he expressed that he lacked the capacity to be an effective leader. This type of fear limits Christians from doing what is either their responsibility, goal, or mission. Scripture provides clarification on this aspect of fear in 2 Timothy 1:7 which states, "For God hath not given us the spirit of fear; but of power, and of love, and of a sound mind."[4] Ministers are quite familiar with these two aspects of fear and countless sermons and biblical texts can be used to define and illustrate these two divergent expressions of fear. Moreover, pastors advise and encourage their people to overcome their negative fears while at the same time fostering a reverential, good fear of the Lord.

In a similar manner, there are two sides to psychological fear. Fear can alert the individual to fight or flee in a dangerous situation. It is a signal to the body for action to preserve the life and welfare of that person faced with threat. Fear sets off an alarm system that mobilizes the body by creating the optimum physiologic conditions for action. Therefore, the heart races to pump blood to all the muscles, breathing is more rapid to deliver oxygen to the body, and there is an outpouring of adrenaline. This is healthy fear, necessary for the preservation of the body. It should operate when a person walks down an alley in a dangerous neighborhood or when a person is approached by an assailant. On a lesser scale, fear or anxiety can mobilize a person to study well for a test or be psychologically prepared for an interview. This healthy, adaptive fear is contrasted with crippling or negative fear. The fear in panic disorder is described as imagined and unrealistic, but nonetheless terrifying. A false alarm that is unnecessary, but paralyzing, rings throughout the brain and body serving no adaptive function and therefore needs to be ameliorated.

The two-sided conceptualization of theological fear and psychological fear is but one example of biblical analogies which approximate secular ones. When taught to patients it may create a real sense of understanding about their illness and in fact, integrates the two worlds in which they dwell. It meshes their psychology with their theology. There are many other examples of integrative work that are beyond the scope of this book. However, in clinical situations, many patients respond well when an attempt is made to integrate theology and psychology. After all, this is what they are trying to do when they are coping with their illness. A minister or even a caring individual attuned to the value of integration will provide much insight and support to the suffering individual. When a person is in the midst of struggling with mental illness, it is far better to identify helpful tools from religion and psychology and/or medicine than to polarize these disciplines.

Other recommendations for the role of the church in assisting its hurting Marthas can be defined and refined. This can be the focus of research and reflection while ministers are in training or in the context of a working church needing to address the problems of its members. Referring back to Kim's story, it was stated that Kim obtained comfort and support from his meeting with other pastors during his difficult time. The therapeutic elements of such meetings are the hallmarks of Christian support, which includes prayer and scriptural sustenance. Can one quantify the therapeutic value of knowing that one's fears and needs are being uplifted in prayer? Given the Christian's belief system, the contribution must indeed be significant. Scriptural sustenance, when used appropriately, is another tool that can be utilized from the realm of theology to assist in a psychological problem. A psychologist, therapist, or psychiatrist would do well to acknowledge how much the church community and its inherent assets have contributed to the progress of their clients and patients. More research and education should be developed in integrating psychology and religion, not merely on a theoretical basis but in a pragmatic framework designed to assist patients.

RESOURCES

Anxiety Disorders Association of America
11900 Parklawn Drive
Suite 100
Rockville, MD 20852
(301) 231-9350

* * *

National Institute of Mental Health
Information Request Line
Parklawn Building
Room 7-99
5600 Fishers Lane
Rockville, MD 20857
(800) 64-PANIC

Chapter 3

Post-Traumatic Stress Disorder:
A Specific Case

Greeting new people in the church was always a thrill of mine. These people are potential new members, new people who could be introduced to God's love and grace or they can be "angels" in our midst. As president of the ladies guild, I often enjoyed inviting the new women to come to our church lunches, our women's meetings, or to my home for a nice dinner. One Sunday morning I spotted a new couple sitting in the back row of our church. The woman was young, in her twenties, thin, and had a pretty, innocent, childlike face. He, on the other hand, was tall, robust, and had very handsome features. They were an attractive couple. I made up my mind to introduce myself to them at the end of the service. As the last hymn was being sung, I slowly made my way to the back of the church. "Hello," I cheerfully said. "My name is Ellen. I'd like to welcome you to our church." The couple smiled and thanked me politely for my greeting. They made an effort to quickly leave the church. I intercepted and asked the woman, "Are you new in town?" She said in a small weak voice, "Yes, we just moved here and I haven't met very many people yet. We're just looking for a church to attend every Sunday." I quickly replied, "Well, you're more than welcome to attend our woman's luncheon. We have it every Tuesday at 11:00. Would you like to join us?" She looked at her husband and then turned to me and said, "I'd like to think about it. Let me get back to you." With this she said good-bye and she and her husband disappeared out of the church.

The following day, I dropped by the church and checked the church registration book and found their names and a telephone number. I came home and gave them a call. She answered and sounded very happy to hear my voice. She stated that she would love to attend the woman's luncheon the next week and asked whether she could bring anything. I said no, and I offered her a lift to the meeting.

At the luncheon, she appeared bright and animated, eager to talk about all sorts of recipes and talk about homemaking ideas. She indicated that she had grown up in a Christian home and had some Bible training as a child. She stated that this luncheon was just the thing she needed in this brand new town. Over the weeks, she continued to attend the meetings and was bright and talkative and motivated to learn about the Bible. She related well to the other women in the group and quickly made many friends. It was about the fifth week when suddenly she stopped appearing at our meetings. In fact, she was absent for the next several meetings and the women's group decided to give her a call. That Sunday, to my surprise, she and her husband were not present at the church as they customarily had been for the past two months. I poked my head into the pastor's office and I asked him whether or not he had seen Deborah and Quentin. He indicated that he had not seen or talked to them. That afternoon I called her number and she answered the phone. I mentioned to her that we were all concerned about her and that we hadn't seen her for awhile. She said that she was sorry that she could not attend the meetings but that she had not been feeling well lately and promised that she would come as soon as she could. I asked whether or not there was anything I could do for her and she replied politely, "No, thank you."

Quite by accident I bumped into Deborah at the supermarket. To my amazement she appeared startled to see me and I noticed that she was wearing quite a bit more makeup than usual. She quickly grabbed several articles of produce, dropped them in her basket, and apologized that she was in a rush. Did I notice a faint limp as she quickly rolled her cart toward the cashier? I felt greatly disturbed, but I didn't understand why.

A couple of months went by and because of the hectic holiday season I had forgotten about Deborah. She had not been present at any of the women's meetings and her church attendance with her husband was sporadic. Periodically, when I did think of her I quickly dismissed the thought and said, "Well, she will be back when she is ready."

One day I received a phone call out of the blue. Deborah was on the phone. She was sobbing. Her voice was shaky and she asked if I could come over. I said yes but asked, "What's wrong?" And she replied, "I think I need some company right now. I'm really worried and upset and I just need somebody to be with me." The two-mile drive didn't take very long but during that time many thoughts went through my head. What could be wrong? What was I about to face? When I knocked at the door it opened a small crack to reveal Deborah huddled by the wall with her hand loosely on the doorknob. She was physically shaking and had a look of fright in her eyes that I had never seen. Her eyes were darting from the door to the living room and back to the door at me again. She appeared like such a frightened animal or even reminded me of a prisoner of war trapped in some horrible cellar. I asked her to sit down and as I held her arm I could feel her shaking in my grasp. She told me that she didn't know what was wrong but she felt that something terrible was going to happen and that she didn't know whether she was going to be able to survive until the next week. She seemed very easily startled by the different household noises and I asked her if she wanted me to fix her something to eat. She replied no, and said she hadn't been able to eat in quite awhile. She mentioned that her appetite and strength seemed to be all gone. As I glanced down, I noticed a big bruise on her leg and I asked her, "How did you get that?" She replied, "Oh, I just fell down the steps; it's just a bad bruise, there are no bones broken."

Deborah admitted that she had been having a lot of bad dreams and that her sleep had been disturbed each night. They were all frightening, violent dreams but she couldn't remember the details. She just wanted someone to be with her to pray with her and comfort her. She felt that everything was doom and gloom and that her future was somehow foreshortened.

The doorbell rang and Deborah jumped up with a start, again cowering by the wall. As she hesitatingly reached to open the door her husband appeared at the entrance. She hurriedly compose herself and greeted him with a kiss. He turned to me, smiled and said in a cordial manner, "What a surprise to have you drop in on us. It is very nice to see you." Deborah offered a half-hearted invitation for dinner but I declined, noticing that the hour was late. There was a vague sense of discomfort in the room and I couldn't shake the way Deborah looked a few moments earlier. I politely said good-bye and headed for home.

My pastor called me on the telephone one day. "Ellen, I just got a call from the hospital. Deborah has been hospitalized. She has had an accident and she asked if you and I could come visit her." I quickly replied, "Yes, I'll be right there" and got dressed and made my way to the hospital where I met the pastor. We went to the orthopedic ward and discovered Deborah in a room, her body bandaged in many areas and a cast on her leg. Her face appeared puffy and bruised and she had a vacant look on her face. As we approached the bed, she turned to us and smiled weakly. She apologized for troubling us and she said she was such an idiot to have been so clumsy. She was, however, very glad that we came to visit her and she seemed comforted that we were in the room although she didn't say very much to us. The nurse came into the room to give her a painkiller and as she drifted off to sleep the pastor and I decided to go out into the hallway. I turned to him abruptly in the hallway and said, "Pastor, there is something seriously wrong with Deborah. And for a while I couldn't figure out what it was. But I think it has something to do with this accident or at least this so-called accident. I don't believe it."

DISCUSSION

This fictional case illustrates the ominous but real problem of abuse as it occurs in the Christian community. It often takes a perceptive individual to recognize the occurrence of abuse because a host of factors can disguise its presence. Deborah, who is the victim of spouse abuse, is experiencing classical symptoms of post-traumatic stress disorder. This disorder represents predictable responses to an extreme stressor that is beyond the scope of usual human experience. These predictable human responses have been well studied in the wartime condition seen in young men called "shell shock." It is not clear why many victims remain in an abusive relationship. Victims may feel trapped and perceive that there are no other options, or feelings of shame may prevent reporting the matter. Various other factors and theories may explain different individual cases.

One of the hallmarks of this disorder is the person develops an amnesia or a psychic numbing as to the event of the abuse. Although repeatedly traumatized, she may be unable to recall various aspects of the physical abuse. In her attempt to avoid the pain of remembering the abuse, she will often proceed with her daily life as if nothing had occurred. But because of the symptoms of post-traumatic stress disorder, which is an anxiety disorder in response to an extreme trauma, she will have a number of physical and psychological manifestations. One such symptom includes recurrent dreams of the trauma as in the case of Deborah, or a victim can experience intrusive thoughts and images of the trauma, so-called "flashbacks." Despite her attempts to avoid anything associated with the trauma, her body may react with physical symptoms resulting from anxiety. Such symptoms would include:

- insomnia
- irritability
- difficulty concentrating
- guardedness
- easily startled

The victim is in tremendous need of medical as well as psychological treatment. Protection from the abuser is mandatory and may require legal maneuvers. The person who suffers from PTSD has a real sense of a foreshortened future. Oftentimes he or she has a sense of estrangement from others. This can make it quite difficult for others to be able to assist in the matter. Often people are not quite sure how to handle these situations. It is important that one become familiar with the various resources within a state where information is available as to how to deal with this crisis. Sources may include hospitals, domestic violence agencies, or abuse hotlines. In some states spouse abuse hotlines may be conducted in English, Spanish, or other languages.

The National Domestic Violence Hotline is an important resource for situations of actual or potential domestic violence. People who call this hotline are provided a safe and confidential opportunity to discuss their fears regarding violence in their home. Abused women are often isolated. Thus, having a twenty-four-hour hotline is invaluable. The hotline is a federally and privately funded resource that serves all fifty states plus Puerto Rico and the Virgin Islands. The organization has an extensive database referral system that can identify crucial services in the victim's local community. This includes domestic violence agencies, counselors, housing, legal services, hospitals, and law enforcement organizations. They will even contact the local police if it is requested by the victim. The local police department is a ready source of help. Some operate sophisticated domestic violence programs. Shelters, particularly those for abused women and children, provide a safe haven as well as access to community resources. The Pacific Garden Mission in Chicago provides food, lodging, clothing, and counseling to many women and children.

Sister Sheila Lyne, Commissioner of Chicago's Department of Health, has implemented the use of the "Abuse Assessment Screen," and "Screening for Domestic Violence in the Emergency Room." These are forms designed to evaluate this problem in the city of Chicago.[1] Using these forms may be an important tool for elucidating and treating the problem of domestic violence.

The American Medical Association has established certain guidelines regarding the handling of victims of domestic violence. National organizations such as the American Red Cross and the National Organization for Victim Assistance (NOVA) can also provide valuable information. In addition to protection for these women, treatment is recommended whether it be in individual counseling with an experienced therapist or support groups.

The Christian community may be at a disadvantage in recognizing situations of abuse. Many are misled by the seeming upright character of the abuser. In a condition where much is kept secret, it would not be surprising that abuse continues unrecognized. It is tragic that abuse can occur in the Christian community. It is unconscionable that it may be ignored. It would serve the church well to be educated about this issue and to assist its helpless members:

> He lies in wait near the villages; from ambush he murders the innocent, watching in secret for his victims.
>
> He lies in wait like a lion in cover; he lies in wait to catch the helpless; he catches the helpless and drags them off in his net.

His victims are crushed, they collapse; they fall under his strength.

He says to himself, "God has forgotten; he covers his face and never sees."[2]

HOW DO CARING CHRISTIANS HELP?

Never assume that domestic violence would not occur in a "Christian home." Domestic violence does occur. Ministers can play an important role in addressing this problem. They may be approached by their church members in a case of suspected abuse and asked to handle the situation. Therefore it is crucial that ministers obtain training in domestic violence and understand the different types of abuse, whether it be physical, sexual, or emotional. They should be informed about the signs and symptoms of battered women and develop a network of social, medical, and legal resources in their community. If they do not have any experience in the matter, they can obtain speakers with expertise to provide workshops in this area. Some churches, especially in metropolitan areas, organize crisis counseling services and support groups for battered women. A minister, aware of the need for these types of services in the community, can be instrumental in instituting these programs, perhaps under the auspices of the church's women's ministries. Under these conditions, training should be provided not only to the minister but also to the counselors who will be assisting battered women.

Caring Christians can play a vital role in recognizing instances of abuse. Look for changes in personality or behavior. An extroverted, friendly woman can suddenly be withdrawn, irritable, or fearful. She may not want to be touched. She may suddenly withdraw from participation in her usual activities, making excuses such as "I am not feeling well." Observe for marked changes in clothing or makeup, all employed to conceal injuries. Look for other behavior changes such as avoiding eye contact with people. Refer to the signs and symptoms of post-traumatic stress disorder, as outlined earlier in this chapter, for further clues.

Many women are secretive about ongoing abuse. A number of factors contribute to their reluctance to confide. Guilt and shame about the abuse, particularly in the Christian environment, keep many women silent. They experience the abuse as humiliating and feel personally responsible for it. Often secrecy is enforced by the spouse who makes threats of repercussion. Threats include potential harm to the wife, abandonment, or suicide. Many women who stay in abusive situations have grown up in a dysfunctional family environment that fosters the perpetuation of abuse as a norm. Unfortunately, some women are silent because previous attempts to confide were ignored.

Because of the secrecy involved in domestic violence, caring individuals should be ready and attentive to listen to the fears of the victim and understand that she may be vague and not easily forthcoming with all the information. She may confide in you on one occasion and then abruptly withdraw for fear of having exposed herself. Because this ambivalence is common, it is important to remain a consistent friend. Many people, when confronted with such a difficult situation, will feel a desire to shy away from the situation. A caring individual should remain consistent and provide safe opportunities for the woman to discuss her predicament. During these talks, you can bolster her self-esteem, which has been terribly damaged. Indicate to her that she is *not* to blame for the abuse. This is a common false perception in battered women. They usually have been told by the abuser and thus believe that they are being beaten because of something they have done. They should be told that physical and sexual abuse is a crime perpetrated by the abuser that is punishable by law.

Strengthen the woman's Christian identity and counsel her that as a "woman of God," she is created to have a loving and respectful relationship with her spouse and is not designed by God to be an object of abuse. When abuse does occur, it reflects a violation of God's standard as well as a criminal act. Caring individuals can provide this type of spiritual instruction. This message can also be reinforced by other teaching programs in the church, including women's Bible studies, marriage workshops, support groups, and sermons.

Ask the victim if she would be willing to speak to the minister or ask for permission to do so on her behalf. Ministers trained in this area can provide counseling or make appropriate referrals. It is possible that the minister can counsel and exercise his or her authority with the husband, however it is important to consider the safety and feelings of the victim. If the woman is afraid to make a move, encourage her to seek counseling at a specialized counseling center for battered women, so she can regain some sense of self-esteem and empowerment to make the necessary changes and leave the abusive situation.

Abusers can also benefit from counseling. Many abusers have issues stemming from their own backgrounds that promote their abusive behaviors. They need to understand these issues and discover a better way of handling their feelings than resorting to abuse. It would be wise to refer such people to therapists trained in this specialized area.

In issues of immediate danger, direct her to local experts in domestic violence. If needed, refer the abused person to a hospital emergency room for medical attention. There, a woman's injuries will be evaluated and documented along with information she conveys as to how she received them. Emergency rooms that follow good guidelines for domestic violence evaluation, such as the one developed by the American Medical Association, will train their staff to ask sensitive questions about domestic violence. This is suspected whenever injuries do not appear to be accidental, especially if they do not match up to the "story" offered by the patient.

Sometimes the pattern of injuries or evidence of sexual abuse can be revealing. Delays in seeking care for significant injuries are also cause for suspicion. An overly protective spouse or one who never leaves the side of the patient may be a clue to the problem. Doctors are encouraged to interview patients in a confidential setting without the presence of the spouse if there is suspected abuse. A woman can choose this time to reveal her abuse. The doctor or hospital staff can then inquire if the woman would like assistance in pressing legal charges against the abuser.

Generally, a woman's sense of her own immediate danger should be taken as a realistic appraisal. Hence, the hospital staff should ask if the woman has friends or family with whom she can stay. If not, she should be referred to a shelter or a safehouse. If none is available, temporary hospitalization for the injuries may be a good alternative while arrangements are being made. A caring individual can provide support for the battered woman as she negotiates these challenging steps.

For information about shelters or safehouses contact your local police department. There may be private as well as public facilities that provide a temporary shelter from danger and offer the victim some protection of identity and location. If the victim is willing, have her contact the police department to determine what recourse she has to ensure safety for herself. If there is evidence of danger to any children in the household, child protective services must be called. Many professionals, including hospital staff, ministers, teachers, and counselors, are mandated by law to contact child protective services in cases of suspected threat to the children. Specific agencies designed to protect children in your locale can be obtained from the police department, schools, or hospitals. You may wish to consult the following organizations for further information.

RESOURCES

National Domestic Violence Hotline
1-800-799-SAFE

This twenty-four-hour hotline will respond to callers from across the nation and will provide crisis intervention that involves giving advice and information geared specifically to the woman's physical and emotional needs at the time of the call. Depending on the situation, they will be directed to the appropriate resource in the woman's region. This may include counseling centers, shelters, state coalitions for domestic violence, etc. In case of extreme emergency, they will be directed to the local police. The hotline maintains an extensive registry of resources throughout the country.

* * *

National Resource Center on Domestic Violence
(800) 537-2238

This organization provides information packets on domestic violence. When you call, you are asked questions to determine your specific informational needs. The appropriate literature will be sent within fifteen business days, or more quickly if requested.

* * *

American Medical Association Coalition
   Against Family Violence
515 North State Street
Chicago, IL 60610
(312) 464-5066

This organization represents a network of physicians sharing information on domestic violence.

* * *

Christian Urban Partnership
90 West Street
Suite 1820
New York, NY 10006
(212) 566-4919

This organization sponsors an annual conference designed to educate Christians on issues of domestic violence, particularly as it can emerge in the church community.

Chapter 4

A Loss for Words: Social Phobia

Felicia, a nurse in the local community hospital, did her job excellently. She was praised for her competent nursing care, her compassion, and her dedication to the service of others. She was active in her local church and participated in many of the women's meetings. Because of her character and her hard work, she was promoted at her job. Part of the requirement of her new status was to teach large groups of nurses in her local community. She was exhilarated by the promotion but quickly became anxious because her new responsibilities required her to speak publicly.

As a child she was always a shy and inhibited girl. It was with great difficulty that she separated from her mother to go to her first kindergarten class. Her period of "adjustment" lasted longer than that of most children. Each morning, Felicia would sit sobbing and refuse to go to school. She would complain of stomachaches or headaches, or throw tantrums, anything to stay home. After a while, she settled down and did quite well throughout her school years. Eventually, Felicia discovered that she had an ability to care for people one-on-one, which prompted her to choose nursing as a profession.

Her recent promotion was the culmination of a great deal of work and something Felicia had yearned for, but she became extremely anxious when her boss discussed her new responsibilities. Her anxiety became overwhelming when she discovered that she had been scheduled to teach her first seminar in six weeks. Felicia panicked as she thought of all sorts of calamities that might occur while she was teaching. She was afraid that she would be at a loss for words. She was also afraid that something terrible would happen. She did not know what it would be, but she was sure that something would cause her tremendous embarrassment and humiliation. Felicia worried constantly about having to speak in public. She agonized over the next six weeks but did her best to prepare her first lesson. Although nursing was Felicia's forte, she suddenly began to feel as if she didn't know the subject at all.

She shared her anxiety with some of the members of her women's group. They all supported her by saying that they understood how intimidating it was to speak in front of large groups, and they all promised to pray for her. Although Felicia drew comfort from their support, she couldn't overcome the feeling of impending disaster.

Felicia recalled that when she trained to become a nurse, she was asked to present a case in front of her peers. She remembered how anxious and worried she felt. In fact, the mere thought of it seemed to make the room spin around her. She recalled the beads of sweat that developed on her brow and her heart pounding like a drum as she stood before her peers. Felicia still found it hard to believe that she was able to get through that presentation so many years ago. She recalled that after it was all over, she promised herself she would never be in a public speaking situation again.

How could this happen? How could she, who was so comfortable in a social setting at work, at home, and in her church, be in such turmoil about speaking before a group of her peers? When she thought about the big picture and what this promotion meant to her, she realized that she was looking at things in a distorted way. How could teaching seminars cause such upset in her life? But she had to admit to herself that it did.

Felicia was now more irritable and distracted when she was with her family. She did not feel the comfort and ease that she normally felt. Her mind was preoccupied with the thoughts of having to teach. She readily admitted her fears to her husband who did his best to reassure her.

Felicia noticed that her fears about public speaking began to affect her attendance at church. Previously she was comfortable in sharing thoughts, ideas, and information at her church meetings. But because of the fears surrounding her new job, she found that she was now also afraid of speaking at church meetings. She had a vague aching notion that she would humiliate or embarrass herself. When she questioned herself as to what she thought might happen, she could not figure it out. Would she stutter in front of everyone and look like a fool? Would she turn beet-red and call attention to herself? Would she be so frightened that she would pass out in front of everybody? Sometimes during the meetings she felt as if her whole body was tense. Her distress was noticeable to her friends and many members of her church.

One day, her pastor approached her and asked if he could speak to her. With a sigh of relief, she walked into his office and began to pour out all the fears that had been troubling her. She indicated that her new job required public speaking—something she was intensely afraid of—and that this fear was beginning to affect other areas in her life. The pastor thought for a moment, and then he stated, "I think I know what you're going through. In fact, earlier in my life, I had to deal with a similar problem. When I was training in the seminary, I discovered that I was fearful of speaking in public settings. It caused me a great deal of pain to think that I was called to be a minister but that I could not feel comfortable preaching from the pulpit. Fortunately, there was help. When I relayed my problems to my professor, he offered to work with me personally in overcoming my phobia. If that didn't help, he said he would recommend someone with professional expertise to address my fear. Although I was very close to dropping out of the seminary, I took him up on his offer. As you can see, it worked."

DISCUSSION

One of the kindest interventions one person can offer to another is an acknowledgement of that person's suffering. When Felicia's pastor empathized with her fears and then proceeded to share his own experience, he accomplished at least two important tasks of a minister. First, he comforted Felicia in letting her know that fear, albeit distorted, can be a normal human emotion and that even "men of God," like himself, can be subject to it. Second, his testimony of his own road to mastery, aided by counseling, provided hope and a solution to Felicia's problem. Testimonies represent a powerful means of support from one Christian to another. In the area of mental health, there are benefits when Christians who have recovered from a psychiatric condition share their experience with another sufferer. The message is conveyed that professional help is available and that emotional difficulties do not mean weak faith or character flaws. This kind of sharing from one Christian to another represents a powerful supportive intervention and plays an important role in the strength of the church community.

Felicia's story demonstrates all the symptoms of a common condition known as "social phobia." Imagined fears of embarrassment and humiliation when required to do public speaking or performing results in the physical and psychological feelings of anxiety. Intense fear and preoccupation with the feared situation occurs. Also problematic are the physical symptoms of anxiety such as palpitations, shaking, stomach upset, dry mouth, and sweating. This often interferes with a person's occupational and social functioning. The person may avoid the feared activity to prevent experiencing the symptoms. When the condition is prolonged and leads to dysfunction, a diagnosis of social phobia is made.

Many of us can appreciate that it is normal for one to have a certain amount of anxiety when a new challenge is presented. On the surface, Felicia's plight does not seem quite so serious. However, if the fear causes prolonged distress and interferes with everyday function, the condition should be evaluated in order to take the next step.

This chapter is not a self-help manual, but there are some practical steps to take. First, one should obtain every opportunity to rehearse or practice the feared activity. In Felicia's case, speaking in front of people is the feared situation. She should progress via gradual steps to reach the goal of public speaking, even if it causes some distress in the beginning. Perhaps she could begin by visiting the lecture rooms. Practicing her lessons alone or with a few trusted friends may be a good start. She could then spend time with the students in smaller groups and graduate to larger ones. Whatever the case, she should not avoid the feared situation. This will only prolong the difficulty of mastery. If this does not afford sufficient progress, she should obtain advice from an expert in social phobia or anxiety disorders. Many university medical centers have stress and anxiety programs. These programs often staff therapists, physicians, and researchers who can do an appropriate evaluation.

Psychological treatments include programs of gradual exposure to the feared situation. The process by which the patient gets used to the situation is called desensitization. The patient is gradually taught through repeated practice and homework assignments, the various techniques and processes required to gain mastery over the fear. Therapy can be done on an individual or group basis depending on the needs of the patient. Medications are sometimes indicated and can prove to be helpful. They are often used just prior to the time of performance and can quell anxiety, palpitations, and the other manifestations of social phobia. Drugs known as beta-blockers, including Inderal (propranolol) and Tenormin (atenolol) can slow down the heart rate and block palpitations. Other medications such as tranquilizers can be used prior to public speaking to calm the emotional aspects of anxiety. Examples include Xanax (alprazolam), Valium (diazepam) or Klonopin (clonazepam), otherwise known as benzodia-zepines. These medications should be used carefully as they may cause sedation. Prolonged use may cause drug dependence, and simultaneous alcohol use must be avoided. However if used properly, under the guidance of a physician, medications can be very helpful to the sufferer.

The very fear of exposing oneself to the distress one experiences from anxiety in social situations makes it hard to seek assistance from others. In general, people with social phobia have to overcome this hurdle before obtaining treatment. Many fail to do so. Acknowledging a problem and seeking appropriate advice paves the road for the Christian to gain mastery. In the Old Testament, the author of Proverbs counsels, "Listen to advice and accept instruction, and in the end you will be wise" (Proverb 19:20). "Make plans by seeking advice; if you wage war, obtain guidance" (Proverb 20:18).[1]

In a sense, Felicia's preparation for her new job is a metaphoric "waging of war." She has to battle her fear, and she recognizes that it has been a lifelong struggle. Under the conditions of this new job, she realizes that her fear will jeopardize her ability to perform if she does not get help. After listening to the pastor's advice, she may choose to seek help or she may ignore his suggestions. If she indeed does have social phobia, in other words, this problem persists to the point where she is not able to carry out her responsibilities, then the wisest approach is to obtain professional help.

Supportive advice from one's own experience as a Christian may begin to help others find answers to their problems. This was done very well by Felicia's pastor. However, there are subtle barriers to providing empathic advice. A major but subtle obstacle is the stigma of having a psychological problem which renders the sufferer unwilling to complain and those who have gone through the experience unwilling to share. It took courage for the pastor to reveal that he had a problem that required psychological help. He had to overcome his own sense of imperfection and the stigma of how he might be viewed by his peers. I once presented the character, "Felicia," at a Christian conference. The audience reacted vehemently to her diagnosis of "social phobia," stating "There's nothing wrong with her. She's absolutely normal." I replied, "That's exactly right. She is *normal*." What did they mean by the word "normal"? Does it mean that Felicia is "normal" because if they were in the same position, they would feel just as anxious? In other words, rather than saying she is "normal," they meant to say she is only being "human." Did they mean that her reaction is not uncommon and would be expected to happen to many in the same circumstance? Did they mean that social phobia is a statistically common condition? Some college students taking a course in "abnormal psychology" begin to view all psychological diagnoses as being abnormal or aberrant. They may even fear that they have the condition they are studying and thus be labeled "abnormal." A judgment value has now been placed on the word "abnormal." It is this notion of normality, that poses confusion in the attempt to treat social phobia. While normalizing anxiety in Felicia's case can be a supportive approach, it should not be used as the excuse to dismiss her complaints and ignore treatment options. Felicia is "normal." She is a normal person, but she has a condition that causes her tremendous distress that would benefit from treatment. In fact, all of the "Marthas" I have written about are normal. Just because they have an anxiety disorder does not mean they are "abnormal." In most people's minds, the stigma of a mental condition causes them to equate the illness with the person, rendering them somehow "abnormal." There are many Marthas serving in our churches and most of them would be grateful if others did not define or judge them by their illness. As for the other definitions of the word "normal," social phobia is a statistically common disorder and, like many psychological conditions, is often missed and therefore untreated. The statement, "Anxiety is normal," meaning that it is "human" and therefore normal, is correct only in the following sense. Anxiety is a normal human emotion and is at times needed to help sharpen us for new challenges or alert us to danger. However, the crippling forms of anxiety that ultimately prevent people from functioning or accomplishing their goals cannot be merely accepted as normal and human. Furthermore, we cannot maintain the belief that since this is "normal," no treatment is needed. If Felicia were to adopt this line of thinking, she might not be adequately prepared for the promotion and might become overwhelmed, anxiety-ridden, and demoralized. If she could no longer work, the question whether her anxiety is normal or not normal will be moot. The important question is "Could she have been helped?" The answer is affirmative.

HOW CHRISTIANS CAN HELP

Facilitate practice sessions or rehearsals for the person with performance anxiety. One of the best ways to desensitize oneself from the fear is to practice in a graduated manner. For example, if Felicia were to feel fairly comfortable in giving her lecture to one or two people, provide her with an opportunity to do so. Or she may start with speaking a few minutes at a time, rather than giving an entire lecture. The next step might be increasing the number in the audience or prolonging the time spent lecturing. These practice sessions can be done among Christians, friends, or family, and should be as frequent as time permits. They should be guided by the person's level of comfort, keeping in mind that there should be increasing levels of difficulty with each step in order to reach the ultimate goal of public speaking at the job site. Christians can do this informally or formally in the church.

Help offset the person's negative self-evaluation that contributes to the fear of humiliation. This chain of thought plagues sufferers with social phobia. Generally, persons are anxious because they are afraid that their presentation will be awful. Presenters worry that they will do something embarrassing or that they may be humiliated by their appearance. They may be afraid of turning beet red, stuttering uncontrollably, or appearing foolish. Persons suffering from social phobia tend to be their own severest critic because they imagine themselves in the worst light. Caring Christian friends can try to understand these imagined negative self-evaluations and challenge them. They can provide encouragement and realistic feedback to the speaker so that he or she does not maintain unreal, pessimistic interpretations. Encouragement and positive feedback are great tools to help in the practice session or in individual conversations with the sufferer. This combined with genuine attempts to improve lecturing will serve the sufferer well.

Think about suggesting professional help. Do not be critical of sufferers; they are genuinely in more distress than most can imagine. Empathize with their suffering to prompt them to seek treatment. Gently help sufferers understand that they have options and should choose the most favorable one. They should not relinquish a much-desired opportunity because of this phobia.

Note how Felicia had made a decision earlier in life never to do public speaking again after her anxiety episode in school. The reason for this is that while she was up in front of the class, she developed physical symptoms of anxiety that are generated by overactivation of the autonomic nervous system. This system, also known as the sympathetic and parasympathetic nervous system, is responsible for the rapid heart rate, sweating, flushing, and sensation of anxiety. When a person leaves the feared activity or situation, there is a decrease in the activity of this system resulting in what the person feels to be an "improvement." Thus, the person has learned that avoidance of such activity reduces the activation of these symptoms. This leads to decisions to avoid. This may be noticed by others, but often it is subtle and unnoticed by friends and family. Unfortunately, this avoidant behavior worsens the phobia as the person never has the opportunity to learn to master fears.

Christians may be able to help by understanding how avoidance behavior is maintained. They can help to point out subtle avoidance practices and encourage exposure to fears. As a person is gradually exposed to the feared activity, the autonomic nervous system is activated and the person will become anxious, but then the anxiety is reduced through a process called "habituation." In other words, a person's nervous system and thought processes adjust to handle the anxiety. This is produced by regular exposure to the feared situation.

Teaching universities with accredited clinical psychology programs can be contacted for help in mastering the fear of public speaking. Many of them operate clinics that are staffed by competent clinicians who also supervise PhD or Doctorate in Psychology students. For social phobia, look for a psychology program that has a strong "cognitive-behavioral" orientation. This tends to be the method of treatment most helpful for phobias. The American Psychological Association has a listing of accredited university clinical psychology programs. Christians can help each other by doing the research in finding appropriate professional help.

For further information and referrals to professionals expert in the "cognitive-behavioral" or "behavioral" orientation in psychology, contact the Association for the Advancement of Behavioral Therapy listed in the resource section at then end of this chapter.

Identification of social phobia and performance anxiety at the educational level provides good training for future pastors. Seminary training requires students to take on a role that involves speaking in public. For most, it is accomplished with training and minimal anxiety. For some, it is a greater obstacle, particularly for those who are prone to be shy or for those who may have some form of performance anxiety or social phobia. Professors and school counselors can play a vital role in identifying these students before they drop out. Because avoidant behavior is common in anxiety disorders, a person suffering from social phobia or performance anxiety will typically react by dropping out without apparent explanation. School advisors, professors, and counselors can help prevent this phenomenon by being alert to the student's concerns and reasons for leaving.

In some seminaries, counseling courses and programs provide a forum to explore issues that cause anxiety among students as well as the general community. These classes provide an opportunity to identify the anxious student who may have performance anxiety as well as other fears. However, this classroom setting would only benefit those students who participate. It will not help the anxious student who does not choose to attend such a class. A more generalized and formalized program to intervene with the anxious seminary student is needed at the dean or advisor level. This is best done in conjunction with the seminary's counseling program or a counseling course instructor. A formalized program attending to these matters may benefit not just the shy, phobic student but others as well.

Be careful not to dismiss a problem by calling it "normal." Although normalizing a behavior is usually supportive, it should not end there. Try to help the person or recommend professional treatment. On the other hand, do not stigmatize or label a person "abnormal" if he or she has intense anxiety. This is a delicate balance but worth exercising in order to help others.

RESOURCES

Anxiety Disorders Association of America
11900 Parklawn Drive
Suite 100
Rockville, MD 20852
(301) 231-9350

* * *

Christian Counseling and Education Foundation
1803 East Willow Grove Avenue
Glenside, PA 19038
(215) 884-7676

Staffed by faculty from Westminster Theological Seminary, this organization provides biblical counseling services. In addition, they provide education and training opportunities through teaching courses at the seminary. These are designed to train the students, pastors, church leaders, and others who are interested in the various aspects of Christian counseling.

* * *

Association for the Advancement of Behavior Therapy
305 7th Avenue
New York, NY 10001-6008
(212) 647-1890

Chapter 5

Generalized Anxiety:
The Individual and the Church

As the teacher of the adult Sunday school, I first met Samuel two years ago. Punctual and solicitous, almost to a fault, he appeared in the Bible study classroom at least fifteen minutes early each Sunday morning. He seemed to relish the study of God's word, and the topics he enjoyed most were church history and the doctrine of law and grace. He was an active participant, and his courteous manner enabled him to relate well to the other adult members of the class. As we all got to know one another better, we found out that Samuel, who was in his thirties, lived with his elderly parents and took care of them. He was single and worked in an office as a bookkeeper. He professed faith in the Lord and had been a Christian for many years.

One day in Bible study, we were discussing the topic of forgiveness. I noticed that Samuel had a worried look on his face. His brow was furrowed, his eyes darted back and forth, and there was a suggestion of tears welling. This was rather unusual for Samuel because he always seemed animated by these discussions and very open about his confidence in God's grace and forgiveness. He looked directly at me at the end of the session and asked whether worrying was a sin. Furthermore, if it were a sin, he wanted to know if constant worrying was due to "weak faith." One by one, the class members addressed their words of comfort and edification, assuring Samuel that "not all worry is sin." Another exclaimed, "if anyone has sinned whether it be in worrying or other matters, God can forgive him if he repents." Since it was the end of the study hour, the class members left after a closing prayer. But it was clear to me that Samuel did not receive any comfort from their words. He was still deeply troubled and sat motionless in his chair. He finally got up and asked if he could speak to me at some convenient time. We agreed to meet for coffee later that afternoon.

At the local diner, Samuel began to pour out his story to me. Between sobs, he told me that he was worried about his parents' aging and frail health. And although there was nothing particularly new about their condition, he feared that they were not going to be there for him for long. Samuel was in fact managing his parents affairs, but felt he couldn't live without his parents' moral support. If they were to die, he feared he would be unable to function. He imagined that he would lose his job and be unable to care for himself. These worries had not always been such a problem but were prominent in the last six months. Smiling a little bit to himself, he said, "Well, I confess that I have always been a worrywart, but I never used to let my worries get to the point where they really affected me. I would simply pray and put these matters into God's hands." Now, however, he was concerned that all his worrying was a reflection of a weak faith. When I indicated that I didn't think so, he seemed momentarily relieved and thanked me for listening to his troubles.

Over the next couple of months, I was on the telephone with Samuel several times a week. He often called repeatedly lamenting that he was worried about his parents' health and his future. I began to realize that he derived temporary comfort from each call but then resumed his worrying. I could not pinpoint anything that led to his worries, and his persistent phone calls and serious ruminations about his future began to annoy me. At times, I became frustrated and exasperated. I felt helpless and unable to do anything for him, and yet he called on me constantly to address his worries. My teaching at the Bible study class became increasingly uncomfortable. I felt trapped by his persistent questioning of God's ability to forgive and to love. His worried, pessimistic state also put a damper on the rest of the class. Gradually attendance dwindled as Samuel began to monopolize the classroom situation. I didn't know how to handle this, so I approached the pastor and the board members for their assistance. Some of them felt that Samuel might be helped if he were actively distracted in doing other things. They tried to develop some responsibilities at church that would keep him busy.

Samuel reluctantly agreed to try out the board's suggestions, but seemed distracted and content assisting the church secretary with some of her duties. His visits to the church office twice a week seemed to fill his time, and he developed a rapport with the secretary. However, gradually as he began to talk to her, he felt comfortable enough to share some of his problems with her. And not surprisingly, the church secretary began to feel bombarded by his persistent worries. After some time, she felt that his presence was impeding her ability to do her work. Although she wanted to be polite, Samuel's volunteer work at the church was beginning to frustrate her as well. She also approached the pastor for help, and once again, he convened with the church board to discuss the situation.

The board wondered how Samuel, who had been a member of their church for such a long time, could have developed into such a problem. They asked each other whether anyone knew about anything in Samuel's life that could be upsetting him so, but nobody had an answer. Some members felt sympathy and compassion for Samuel and stated that this was a matter of being patient. Others who were more in direct contact with him guiltily expressed their feelings of frustration and helplessness. Still others were quite open in expressing their anger and felt that something should be done quickly. The pastor stated that this was a complicated situation, and he asked if a visit to Samuel's parents might not be a good idea. Not knowing what else to do, the board members agreed that it was worth a try. The pastor made plans to visit Samuel's parents, but admonished the board, "If the feelings that are being generated in this church continue, I fear that Samuel will not stay in our midst for long. It would not take long for Samuel to sense the frustration of his peers and leave our church. I want you all to understand this because I've seen it happen again and again."

DISCUSSION

"So that there should be no division in the body, but that its parts should have equal concern for each other. If one part suffers, every part suffers with it; if one part is honored, every part rejoices with it. Now you are the body of Christ, and each one of you is a part of it."[1]

When mental illness occurs in the church, everyone is affected. Scripture supports this and tells us that as a body, we not only rejoice together but at times we suffer together especially when one member is hurting. A difficult and challenging problem confronting many pastors and lay leaders is what to do when one member is afflicted with psychological problems which then impact negatively on other members. Hopefully, education and increased awareness of the disorder would develop sensitivity and insight into the problem. This combined with the biblical exhortation to work as a body may make the church one of the best support networks for people afflicted with anxiety.

Samuel is suffering from generalized anxiety disorder. His problem is identified by the fact that he has been suffering from excessive worry for the past six months. These worries center around his aging parents as well as his ability to sustain his job should they die. Although there is no evidence for the immediacy of his fears, he finds that his worries are excessive and difficult, if not impossible to control. Interestingly, he alludes to this, showing some insight when he labels himself as always being a "worrywart." However, even he has noticed that in the past six months his worries are getting out of hand. Oftentimes, people with generalized anxiety disorder find that they are unable to control their worries and that these worries become pervasive and eventually affect their ability to function socially or occupationally. Certainly, if it doesn't affect their ability to function, generalized anxiety disorder may cause severe distress. This disorder is also characterized by associated symptoms such as restlessness or feeling keyed up, easy fatiguability, difficulty in concentration, muscle tension, or some form of sleep disturbance. If you were to ask Samuel about any of these features in the past six months, he would be likely to report that on many days he experiences shakiness, tension in his muscles, and feels tired. He might also report that sometimes at work his "mind has gone blank," which then contributes to his worries that he may lose his job. This then becomes a vicious cycle as he begins to dwell on a series of catastrophic thoughts—his parents dying, poverty after losing his job, and the inability to support himself. Sufferers from this disorder pose a dilemma in the church setting. Many times the excessive worry of such people develops a life of its own and has significant effects on church activities, such as the monopolization of Bible studies or of people's time with discussions of excessive worries and the demands for reassurance. This may be a source of frustration and anger for the church members. Many people who do not suffer from this problem find it difficult to understand or even tolerate the excessive worries of their fellow church member. They attempt to reassure the person with biblical truths but are exasperated when this yields only temporary results and the patient reverts back to his worrisome thinking.

It is important to understand that such people find it difficult to control their worries and that this is a hallmark for the disorder. It is not only an individual problem but begins to be a problem for the entire church body. After several board meetings in Samuel's church, the pastor recognized that the negative reactions Samuel's problem generated among his peers could lead to potential ostracism. Therefore, recognition and a better understanding of this problem is mandatory for the health of the individual as well as the life of the church. One can see that Samuel's church has made numerous thoughtful attempts to help Samuel's situation. It is these kinds of interventions that contribute to the welfare and the support that is provided by a church when a person experiences a crisis in his or her life. Such interventions may on their own sustain such a person until he or she is able to overcome the symptoms of generalized anxiety disorder. However, there may be a point for some individuals where professional help is warranted.

Psychological treatments for generalized anxiety disorder exist at this point in time. However, the diagnosis of generalized anxiety disorder warrants further study and research. We know less about its familial aspects, biological features, or even its symptom manifestations than we do about other anxiety disorders. Even so, it is quite clear that numerous individuals have benefitted from psychological treatment. Additionally, individuals may also benefit from psychiatric and medical evaluation as there are many other illnesses that can occur in the presence of generalized anxiety disorder or mimic its features. Once recognized, these other disorders can then be treated. Such disorders include clinical depression, adjustment disorders, substance abuse, or even medical conditions that result in anxiety. In children there is a form of generalized anxiety disorder called "overanxious disorder of childhood." The childhood form of the disorder closely resembles the adult form. All these conditions are amenable to treatment and the benefits of improved functioning are valuable.

HOW CHRISTIANS CAN HELP

By way of "prescriptive" information for the church leader, we can extract important lessons from Samuel's case.

Caring people made the effort to listen to Samuel's misery, sharing in the burden, and then praying for him. No doubt, caring people made multiple attempts to comfort him. Proverbial wisdom teaches us that kind words are capable of cheering a man whose heart is weighed by anxiety (see appendix). Although the effect is temporary, it still helps.

The church members involved with Samuel were honest with their own feelings of frustration, which facilitated discussion with their pastor about the possible ramifications of these resentments. They convened as often as needed in a group, employing problem-solving approach and prayer. Hopefully, one of the issues they addressed was how to minister to Samuel without sacrificing the viability of the Sunday school class or the functions of the church secretary. They offered Samuel a place to work and occupy spare time.

Caring people made efforts to do more fact-finding to help Samuel. The pastor offered to visit the parents. What else can a concerned caregiver do?

Caring people continue to listen, even when it feels as if nothing is changing. They continue to provide a "listening ear" believing that the process alone will be experienced as supportive, even if no solutions are offered. Caring people do not necessarily look to a quick fix, hoping that the person will not complain any further. In matters such as generalized anxiety disorder, there is rarely a quick solution.

Caring people acknowledge their own limitations and the roles they play. They forsake the accolades of being the hero to solve a person's problem and direct the sufferer to appropriate sources of help, yet remain with him once he finds help. One minister reported that when a particular member experienced a change in mood, he often asked if the congregant had had a recent medical checkup. Sometimes, a person supposedly suffering from generalized anxiety disorder has a physical condition that manifests itself initially with mood changes. A checkup would reveal whether or not this is the case. When they realize professional help is warranted, caring people make the referral even at the risk of offending the individual or being spurned. In Samuel's case professional psychological help would be beneficial. Appropriate treatment along with the supportive resources of the church should pave the road for a good outcome.

RESOURCES

Focus on the Family Program
Colorado Springs, CO 80995
(719) 531-3400 Ext. 2700

* * *

American Psychiatric Association
Division of Public Affairs
Department MM99
1400 K Street NW
Washington, DC 20005
(888) 357-7924

* * *

Center for Christian Psychological Services
Lutheran Brotherhood Building
2780 Snelling Drive North Suite 104
St. Paul, MN, 55113
(651) 633-5290

Chapter 6

Phobia: The Simple Is Complicated

Dr. Charles Connolly was a successful ophthalmologist of African-American descent. He was raised in a Christian home and always felt that he was called to go into the mission field. After finishing medical school and graduating with honors, he entered into specialty training in ophthalmology. He was a skilled physician and quickly earned the respect of his colleagues. When he graduated, he established a successful practice. He was also given an appointment at a university hospital where he was engaged in teaching medical students as well as doing research.

Charles had never forgotten his dream of serving as a medical missionary, but because of the demands of his ophthalmology practice and his involvement in the university hospital, he felt that he had to delay his aspirations of serving the Lord abroad. He envisioned that at some point in his career he would need to make a major life decision in order to enter the mission field.

Life went very smoothly for Charles Connolly, and he was very active in a local Christian church. Soon, he met a lovely woman whom he married. After several years, he became the father of two children, and in many respects, his life was quite fulfilled. Maintaining an active interest in the missions committee of his church, he often investigated and reported on various missionary activities to the church members and invited their support. He shared his dreams of the mission field with his family, and his wife was extremely supportive.

One year, Charles was attending a regional retreat where he learned of a specialized medical organization that went abroad to various countries to assist in the extensive health needs of the underserved. These ships transported doctors, nurses, medical supplies, and operating room facilities to various ports internationally and would provide professional care for the indigent population. Intrigued by this particular mission program, Charles requested more information. He was delighted and surprised to hear that they were looking for an ophthalmologist to serve among the population in Africa where there was an alarming high rate of eye diseases. In fact, they were desperately looking for an ophthalmologic surgeon to address these needs. Would Dr. Connolly be available at any time? This was the chance of a lifetime.

Charles recognized that he finally had to make the difficult decision. He would have to leave his practice and the comfort of his professional community to fulfill his dream. Yes, there was a lot of personal sacrifice to be made. On the other hand, this was the challenge that he had always desired. Since he was a young boy, Charles prayed that the Lord would send him to the mission field. After much prayer and discussion with his wife and members of his church, Charles Connolly elected to apply to this mission organization. Within a period of two weeks, he received an acceptance letter. He and his family would be sent abroad within three months time. Things were moving very quickly for Charles and his family. They set forth to plan all the details of their move and began saying good-bye to all their friends and family. Things seemed to be going quite smoothly for the family. Although their schedules were very busy, they looked forward with anticipation to their new environment. There were going to be new schools, responsibilities, a new home, and many challenges to meet.

It was during this time of preparation that Charles awoke one day from a frightening dream. In it, he was attacked by a large coiling snake. He awoke from his nightmare, soaked in perspiration and began to recall his childhood fear of snakes. He had almost forgotten about this phobia, and in fact, it had receded into the back of his mind. After all, how many snakes does one become exposed to in a large city? Now his fear reappeared. Realizing that he would most likely be sent to places where snakes were endemic to the area, he became frantic. How utterly ridiculous, he rationalized, that a simple fear like this could actually rob him of the joy of his plans to go abroad! But the more he thought, the more fearful he became. In fact, now the anticipation of sailing abroad on this medical mission project was overshadowed by consternation and worry. The thought of snakes and the fear of being bitten by them became Charles' major preoccupation. His wife noticed that his preparations for the trip began to lose their fervor and excitement. In fact, her husband seemed reluctant to talk about the trip. This was rather perturbing for her, and she decided to confront him.

DISCUSSION

Charles Connolly is suffering from a classic case of a specific phobia or what was once called a "simple phobia," in this case the fear of snakes. Many people suffer from different forms of phobias—the sight of blood or injury or a fear of animals, objects, or certain situations. The latter can include the fear of driving or the fear of flying. Phobias cause intense anxiety characterized by physical symptoms such as sweating, palpitations, muscle tension, and gastric symptoms. Even though it is still problematic for them, generally, adults do recognize that their fears are exaggerated. Children, on the other hand, often see their fears as being realistic and posing a real danger. Many people suffer from unrecognized phobias. They are usually not a problem unless they interfere with functioning, such as performance at work, interaction in social situations, or the general quality of life. Phobias are intense fears that last for at least six months and oftentimes more.

In Charles Connolly's case, his phobia was not a problem until the call to the mission field. It then became the stumbling block for his ability to participate in the mission program comfortably, if at all. At this point in his life, his fears may represent a diagnosable phobia, particularly if it persists.

Psychological treatments are available for phobias. Oftentimes these include a desensitization program targeted at the feared trigger whether it be situations, objects, or other stimuli. These treatments can assist the phobic patient in coping with the feared stimulus and give him gradual tolerance of the situation or item feared. It teaches him not to avoid his fear, but to expose himself to it in a gradual way in order to master it. Without treatment, most people tend to handle their phobias by avoidance. In some cases, people endure the feared stimulus and are extremely distressed at having to do so. Avoidance can be detrimental to a person's life and most certainly hinders treatment. Unable to pursue interests that he or she would ordinarily pursue, the phobic person leads a very restricted lifestyle.

Paul's experience as recorded in Scripture offers encouragement: "For when we came into Macedonia, this body of ours had no rest, but we were harassed at every turn—conflicts on the outside, fears within. But God, who comforts the downcast, comforted us by the coming of Titus."[1] Notice that Paul did not refrain from his work despite the "fears" and the "conflicts" and being "harassed." Observe that God provides comfort, in this case in the person of Titus. Perseverance, bolstered by confidence in God's comfort will combat the tendency to avoidance. It is also a prerequisite for good response to psychological treatments in which a patient practices exposure to his or her fears in order to gain mastery. For many Christians, mastering a phobia begins by acknowledging the fear to themselves and to God in the following manner: "Do not be anxious about anything, but in everything, by prayer and petition, with thanksgiving, present your requests to God. And the peace of God, which transcends all understanding, will guard your hearts and your minds in Christ Jesus."[2]

The goal of treatment is to enable persons such as Charles Connolly to overcome fear in order to pursue important ministries.

HOW THE CHURCH CAN HELP

Facilitate treatment. Given that psychological treatments such as gradual desensitization work for specific phobias, it would be extremely beneficial for the church or its mission board to facilitate treatment as part of the preparation for the missionary. This may take the form of obtaining an appropriate counselor such as the network of trained therapists that specialize in working with church or missionary organizations. Financial support for the treatment is a very positive form of support. It obviously offers the concrete benefit of paying for the services, particularly at a time when the missionary is prepared to sacrifice his current source of income to serve abroad. In paying for the treatment, the church or mission board provides confirmation and meaning to the idea that this psychological treatment is part of the training program for missions and that the church is helping to equip the missionary for service. As a consequence, it destigmatizes the process of getting mental professional help.

Behavioral/desensitization treatment for specific phobias is relatively short term in length. This is of practical importance as Charles Connolly has three months before he travels abroad. This is a realistic time frame for this type of therapy. During this period, the mission board could optimize results by collaborating with the therapist, each playing a unique but interdependent role in helping the patient. The psychological treatment is intended to handle the phobia in an effort to get the patient to go abroad with some level of comfort. In meeting this goal, the therapist addresses the patient's phobic avoidance that may deter his plans.

Apart from the specific phobia, there are many other issues that do arise when one is preparing for the mission field. These factors can be logistical, psychosocial, and spiritual. These issues can be handled more effectively by the mission board or the church. Hence, collaboration between the mission board and the therapist would define how each component can contribute to assist the person in preparation for the mission field.

This case illustration hints at two other questions that need to be addressed. Does Charles Connolly have concerns about his ability to perform in his new environment? For example, does his dream reflect anxious concerns about how he will do, especially in light of the radical changes that he and his family will be experiencing? The second question is: Does Charles have concerns or beliefs in the role of spiritual oppression and its affect on his endeavor? These questions warrant exploration and are often best handled by those who have experience in preparing missionaries. There are so many issues that may be troubling Charles which need articulating. It certainly would be valuable for him to have a confidant in the church, someone with whom he feels comfortable in sharing his misgivings and anxiety. It would help him to identify for himself those areas where he feels inadequate and provide an opportunity for a caring Christian to give him a listening ear, prayer support, and guidance. The spiritual confidant should be someone of Charles's own choosing. Preferably, he or she should also be capable of understanding the issues related to mission work and the adjustments that are required. This person can be seen as a partner in the venture, helping to understand all the variables involved in order to seek the success of the mission. Didactic training provided by the sponsoring missionary organization in the form of language preparation classes, cross-cultural training, and workshops designed to impart important facts are invaluable. These can be tailored to address Charles Connolly's particular needs and concerns.

The second question raised by this case illustration has to do with Charles's fears of spiritual oppression. The definition of this entity can be ambiguous. However, it generally refers to opposition by spiritually evil forces against the work of a Christian. It is beyond the scope of this text to define the meaning and nuances of this matter. Suffice it to say, that spiritual oppression is thought to play a thwarting, discouraging role among many Christians who are about to embark on difficult but potentially life-changing ministries. Therefore, the mission board must answer the question as to whether the potential missionary is equipped with the strengths, talents, and personality profile needed to sustain the obstacles. One needs to keep in mind that although this has been a lifelong vision for Charles Connolly, it is not clear that the mission field represents the optimum setting for him. In order to find out, he may do well by venturing out and doing this work on a short-term basis. Where possible, he should not completely sever his current professional responsibilities, but maintain a clear opportunity to return. For example, taking a sabbatical from work to explore missions is a means to see if one can be a full-time missionary without cutting off established options. Short-term missions may provide the best means of keeping one's options open, and thus reduce the anxiety that accompanies major life changes. At some point in the future, when adjustments have been made and experience is gained, the person can make a full-time commitment to the mission field.

Encourage the wife and family as part of the missionary team. Until now, we have been looking at Charles Connolly's psychological, spiritual, and career issues. In addition, it is of vital importance to examine the issues and concerns of the wife and the family to see if there are any concerns and anxieties that have not been addressed. It is not a simple matter of Charles's phobia but a whole host of unverbalized concerns from the family members must be addressed. The church and mission board need to be attentive to family issues and equally strong support should be provided. Viewing the family as a unit or a mission team can be an affirming stance. After all, the family is the one important constant in a setting where there are many new changes to face. Therefore, the family can be taught to provide support for one another. The family can be prepared by the church or mission board for the possible obstacles each member may face and learn how to handle them.

RESOURCES

Association for the Advancement of Behavior Therapy
305 7th Avenue
New York, NY 10001-6008
(212) 647-1890
www.aabt.org/aabt

The Association for the Advancement of Behavior Therapy is a not-for-profit membership organization of mental health experts who use behavior therapy and/or cognitive-behavior therapy to gain a better understanding of human behavior and then use this understanding to help others accomplish specific changes or goals. Individuals seeking a behavior therapist can either use the Web site or send a self-addressed, stamped, business-size envelope, and AABT will send a list of professionals practicing in your state who participate in the Clinical Directory along with a copy of its *Guidelines for Choosing a Behavior Therapist* pamphlet and, if available, a fact sheet for the problem for which treatment is being sought.

* * *

Anxiety Disorders Association of America
11900 Parklawn Drive
Suite 100
Rockville, MD 20852
(301) 231-9350

* * *

Link Care Center
1734 West Shaw Avenue
Fresno, CA 93711
(800) 794-5920
www.linkcare.org

This is a nondenominational, Christian organization developed in 1965 to provide services for missionaries and missionary candidates. Their goal is to prepare missionaries and their families through education, supportive intervention, and counseling services. They maintain a staff of psychologists, marital and family therapists, as well as pastoral counselors to address these various needs.

In addition they perform missionary candidate assessments for many mission boards. This assessment involves a detailed interviewing process with a psychologist who performs a battery of psychological tests. This is done to evaluate a person's appropriateness for missions as well as potential problems if he were to go into the mission field. The Link Care Center also conducts conferences that address cross-cultural and linguistic issues for those who are interested. These are held at scheduled times during the year.

* * *

American Psychological Association
750 First Street NE
Washington DC 20002
(800) 964-2000 (APA Referral)
(202) 336-5500
www.apa.org

Chapter 7

Depression:
"An Illness, Not a Weakness"

Lily is a forty-nine-year-old church member who has always been active in the Ladies' Guild, serving in many capacities. She is a warm, friendly woman who often can be relied on to show hospitality to visiting missionaries as well as church members. She has always devoted herself to caring for her family. Her children are now young adults who are beginning to pursue lives of their own. One day Lily's daughter called Maria, a friend of the family, and told Maria that she was worried about her mother. It appeared that Lily did not seem her usual cheerful self, and in fact, did not bother to get out of bed many mornings of the week. She also appeared tired, withdrawn, and often burst into tears unprovoked.

Maria gave Lily a call. When she explained the reason for her call and her concern, Lily seemed somewhat embarrassed and stated that nothing was really wrong. Lily was recently sick with the flu and thought she was just tired. Maria agreed to pray for her, offering to help in any way she could. However, after hanging up, Maria did not feel she really connected with Lily.

A week later, Lily called Maria and confessed that she was having problems with her family. She felt terribly anxious and irritable. Lily continued to talk about her family and how upset she was with them. Her friend listened patiently, asking questions occasionally. Lily finally admitted, "I think there is something wrong with me."

DISCUSSION

Clinical depression is a common disorder, affecting anywhere from 10 to 25 percent of women and 5 to 12 percent of men at some point in their lives, indicating that it is twice as common in women.[1] It is often unrecognized and untreated. This is perhaps due to the stigma of having a mental health problem that exists both in the Christian and non-Christian community. This is unfortunate as there are many good treatments for depression.

The consequences of this disorder are major. Depression often impairs one's ability to perform at work, which may lead to job loss and prolonged unemployment. Disturbances in marital and family relationships can occur as well as in social and church relationships. Depressed persons are vulnerable to social isolation. Drug and alcohol abuse may result because depressed people may self-medicate to treat their terrible feelings. There may be increased physical complaints such as headaches, lethargy, and many other vague symptoms causing excessive visits to the medical doctor.

Recognizing the signs and symptoms of depression is the first step in meeting the challenges posed by this major health problem. A constellation of symptoms occurs beginning with almost constant depressed mood or irritability for at least a two-week period. In addition, a sleep disturbance often occurs, characterized by early morning awakening or multiple awakenings during the night. Others complain that they sleep too much. Often there is a decrease in appetite with weight loss. However, in some people increased eating may occur, accompanied by weight gain. The depressed person often feels excessively tired and unable to concentrate. Some complain of intense anxiety or are worried about their physical health. Their thoughts may center on feelings of self-worthlessness, guilt that is often unrealistic, negative outlook on the future, and death. As a result, they may withdraw from their family and friends. They often lose their ability to enjoy things that were previously enjoyable. Depressed persons may experience periods of spontaneous crying although some describe an overwhelming sense of sadness but are unable to cry.

One of the best biblical pictures of depression is found in Psalm 88, attributed to Heman. Many of the symptoms of depression are described poignantly in this psalm. Although not confirmed in the psalm, some speculate that the writer may have suffered from leprosy. Nonetheless, Psalm 88 speaks of the feelings and thoughts of an afflicted individual, a sufferer who reveals his misery to God. This psalm can be helpful to the suffering individual who can identify with the author, but it is by no means a cure. The psalm serves best to assist loved ones and caregivers in understanding the mind-set of the depressed individual. Understanding is a step toward empathy:

> O Lord, the God who saves me, day and night I cry out before you.
> May my prayer come before you; turn your ear to my cry.
> For my soul is full of trouble and my life draws near the grave.
> I am counted among those who go down to the pit; I am like a man without strength.
> I am set apart with the dead, like the slain who lie in the grave, whom you remember no more, who are cut off from your care.
> You have put me in the lowest pit, in the darkest depths.
> Your wrath lies heavily upon me; you have overwhelmed me with all your waves. Selah
> You have taken from me my closest friends and have made me repulsive to them. I am confined and cannot escape; my eyes are dim with grief.
> I call to you, O Lord, every day; I spread out my hands to you.

Do you show your wonders to the dead? Do those who are dead rise up and praise you? Selah

Is your love declared in the grave, your faithfulness in Destruction?

Are your wonders known in the place of darkness, or your righteous deeds in the land of oblivion?

But I cry to you for help, O Lord; in the morning my prayer comes before you.

Why, O Lord, do you reject me and hide your face from me?

From my youth I have been afflicted and close to death; I have suffered your terrors and am in despair.

Your wrath has swept over me; your terrors have destroyed me.

All day long they surround me like a flood; they have completely engulfed me.

You have taken my companions and loved ones from me; the darkness is my closest friend.[2]

From the symptomatic description of clinical depression provided earlier, many are recounted by the psalmist. He "cries out to the Lord day and night," indicating he is depressed and clues the reader that he may be suffering from insomnia. His "life draws near the grave" is a lament that his thoughts are centered upon death. He reports excessive fatigue when he remarks that he is "like a man without strength." His withdrawal from others is evident when he blames God for "taking him from his closest friend." Anxiety is revealed when he claims that "Your terrors have destroyed me."

These six symptoms of depression are fairly convincing if one trains oneself to look for them. If not persuaded, one then can hypothetically ask the psalmist or realistically ask a person reminiscent of the psalmist the following questions: Is your appetite disturbed? Do you have trouble concentrating? Do you feel tremendously guilty or worthless? Do you find that nothing gives you any pleasure anymore? According to specialists, only five of the above symptoms inclusive of depressed mood or loss of pleasure are needed to make the diagnosis of clinical depression. Yet it is remarkable how often the diagnosis is missed by peers and professionals. It is not surprising that the majority of depressions in this country are not treated.

Because depression can wreak such havoc in all areas of a person's life, it is important to pursue treatment. Overcoming the stigma and ignorance surrounding depression is a challenge to the secular as well as the church community. One needs to overcome false ideas such as, "The person is depressed because he does not have enough faith." This can be damaging as the depressed person already has a propensity for excessive guilt and would easily be convinced that his or her faith is inadequate. Rather, he or she should be encouraged to seek help, much in the way that if one had pneumonia or diabetes one would seek medical attention. Many depressions are just as biologically based as pneumonia or diabetes.

Similar to the false idea that insufficient faith is responsible for depression is the notion that depression is a direct result of excessive personal sinning. When someone appears to be suffering from depression, it is generally counterproductive to blame that person by telling him or her that the depression is a punishment for sin. The counseling Job received from his friend is an example of such misleading interpretation. Depressed people will often unnecessarily take the blame, express repentance for some unknown sin and venture no further to seek help. They remain unaware of the biological basis of depression.

Brain chemicals such as serotonin and norepinephrine have been found to be disturbed in clinical depression. That is why for some patients, correcting these brain chemicals with medications such as Tofranil (imipramine), Zoloft (sertraline), Pamelor (nortriptyline), Prozac (fluoxetine), and many others will dramatically improve the depression. It also explains why some depressions have a familial tendency and that for some reason some people are genetically vulnerable to depression just as others are genetically vulnerable to migraines or ulcers. It can occur and recur under conditions of stress or spontaneously. Because clinical depression does not manifest itself in visible symptoms such as a rash, or a finding such as an elevated blood pressure, or in an abnormal blood test, many find it difficult to recognize depression when it occurs. The manifestations are largely in thought processes and behavior that serves to disguise its biological origins. It is labeled as "emotional," without understanding that many emotional symptoms have biological causes.

What are the sources of help for the depressed individual? A consultation with a specially trained physician such as a psychiatrist can determine the presence of clinical depression. Other professionals such as psychologists, trained social workers, and Christian counselors who have expertise in evaluating depressions, may provide needed information. If medication is required only a medical doctor can prescribe it. A family physician should be consulted for two reasons. One is to make sure that the person's physical examination is normal and that he or she does not have a medical illness that mimics depression, and the other reason is to obtain a referral to the appropriate mental health professional in the community. Clergymen may have information about local physicians and other professionals whom they recommend. If the above are not available, medical centers and hospital psychiatric departments may be helpful through their referral network. In addition, Christian organizations such as Focus on the Family, has a counseling department which provides information and referrals from their extensive registry of Christian counseling professionals throughout the United States. They can be reached at the address and telephone number printed in the resource section at the end of this chapter. Also, the American Psychiatric Association based in Washington, DC, has district branches that may provide listings of board-certified psychiatrists. See the resource listing at the end of this chapter for address and telephone number.

Lily's condition may seem vague and unclear on first look. But on closer inspection, there are clues to her depression— spontaneous crying, irritability, anxiety, withdrawal, tiredness and even her own determination that, "there's something wrong with me." All this should be taken seriously. From a spiritual point of view, sufferers require reassurance that although they may be preoccupied with an overwhelming sense of guilt and weakness from the depression, their God will carry them through this trial just as He would any other. The goal is to facilitate their getting appropriate help in order to take care of the body (and mind) that God has given them. In order not to place a judgment value on the condition, it is important to remember that "Depression is an illness, not a weakness."[3]

A special type of depression warrants description. This is called major depression, postpartum type, or more familiarly known as "postpartum depression." Because it is frequently unrecognized and therefore untreated, the following illustration is presented to provide a greater understanding of this condition.

Mr. Questra, a first-time father, appears at your door, looking weary and haggard and asks to speak to you concerning his wife. He relates that Mrs. Questra has just berated him miserably and asked him to leave the house. Complaining that he was lazy and unhelpful with their newborn, that he did not complete all the preparations necessary for the baby's arrival, and that he was inattentive and insensitive to her feelings, she broke out into fits of sobbing and demanded that he leave. Mr. Questra was confused. He had never seen his wife this way and sought out his pastor for help.

Three weeks ago, after a difficult delivery, Mrs. Questra gave birth to a normal, healthy girl. She thought it was strange that she did not feel as joyful about the event as she anticipated. In fact, she noticed that she was very anxious about the baby's health and her own health, and was preoccupied with these thoughts all the time. Nighttime was dreadful as she ruminated over fears about whether she was a good mother and whether the baby's crying meant that there was something terribly wrong. Insomnia plagued her daily, and she could not eat as her stomach was "tied in knots" from worry.

Mr. Questra tried very hard to help his wife, but she did not seem to notice or appreciate his efforts. He took time off from his job and even obtained around-the-clock help from his sisters. Nothing seemed to cheer or distract his wife. He was at his wits end.

You decide to visit the couple at their home the next day, and after an initial awkward silence, Mrs. Questra becomes distracted by the baby's cry. She appears very uncomfortable and exclaims that she is unfit to be a mother.

Postpartum depression occurs in approximately 10 to 15 percent of all deliveries.[4] It is often not recognized when it occurs in the church community. Yet it is a common illness that occurs in the life of a woman. It causes tremendous emotional pain in the mother that can impact on mother-infant bonding and may lead to impaired cognitive development of the child. It often wreaks havoc on the marital relationship as well as impacts on other children in the family.

Recognizing the presence of postpartum depression is extremely important. Many should share in this responsibility, including the affected woman, doctors, nurses, childbirth educators, family members, and also the church community. The latter represents a large circle of concerned individuals who may have had similar experiences and may be able to share in the psychological support and spiritual encouragement. They can also prompt each other to seek treatment when necessary. In addition, they can provide assistance with childcare responsibilities while the mother is afflicted.

What are the symptoms of a postpartum depression? First, one needs to distinguish "depression" from "postpartum blues," which is a temporary condition after childbirth unlike clinical depression. Postpartum blues usually last for a few days after delivery, characterized by crying spells, irritability, and mood instability. It happens frequently after delivery and is assumed to result from the rapid hormonal changes after birth. The key feature is that it resolves spontaneously after a few days. On the other hand, postpartum depression represents a persistent depressed mood lasting for two weeks or longer. During this time, the woman is depressed most of the day, and there is a loss of pleasure. In addition, she may suffer from insomnia (even when the baby is sleeping), change in appetite (significant increase or decrease), anxiety regarding her own health or the welfare of the child, fatigue, or recurrent thoughts of death. An unusual form of depression that represents a psychiatric emergency occurs when the woman also experiences a break with reality demonstrated by auditory or visual hallucinations or delusions. The latter may include thoughts such as "the child is possessed by the devil." Immediate psychiatric attention and often hospitalization is warranted as both the safety of the child and the mother are at risk because of the mother's delusional perceptions. This condition is called postpartum psychosis.

Risk factors for postpartum depression include a previous history of depression (postpartum or nonpostpartum), family history of depression or alcoholism, poor early childhood environment, unwanted pregnancy, a complicated labor and delivery, poor obstetrical outcome (birth defects), or marital discord. If these factors exist, one should consider oneself at risk, and timely counseling and support should be obtained. However, many women develop postpartum depression even without risk factors, and therefore, if these symptoms develop they should pursue treatment.

Treatment is effective in postpartum depression and often includes using antidepressant medication, individual psychotherapy, marital or family counseling, or group support. In some cases, hospitalization, antipsychotic medication, or electroconvulsive treatments may be needed. Because treatments are effective and the consequences of untreated depression are major, women should be encouraged to seek help to relieve the distress of this debilitating condition.

HOW THE CHURCH CAN HELP

The church can be instrumental in helping the mother with postpartum depression. It can provide a strong network of support for these suffering women until they regain their emotional health.

Supporting the mother. Assist the mother in getting professional help if she has not done so yet. Generally, postpartum depression responds well to medication, so a psychiatrist would be a good choice for obtaining care. The obstetrician should be told of any symptoms described previously at the postpartum checkup, which generally occurs six weeks after birth. He or she can be a good referral source for psychiatric attention.

Provide ample babysitting for the mother as needed. She will need time for herself either to rest or simply to attend to her own needs. Certain antidepressant medications may be sedating, so that help for the care of the baby needs to be arranged. Keep in mind that a balance is needed between providing extra help in caring for the baby and encouraging mother-infant bonding.

One common characteristic of postpartum depression is intense anxiety experienced by the mother. She is often overwhelmed by concerns over the welfare of the child and her own health. The mother is plagued with a great deal of doubt about herself and her mothering ability. Women who have gone through this process can provide reassurance to the new mother.

The church can provide ongoing support groups for young mothers. Being the mother of an infant or young children can be a stressful and isolating experience. It is worse for those women who suffer from postpartum depression. The church community has the resources to diminish these burdensome conditions by providing opportunities for young mothers to meet on a regular basis. Their identified purposes for meeting can center on multiple themes such as Bible study, prayer meeting, weekly luncheons, or educational workshops. The latter should incorporate topics relevant to young mothers such as Christian parenting, the healthy marriage, understanding relationships, the role of prayer, overcoming depression, or any other issue that is relevant to the members of the group. To facilitate these groups, many topical study guides and Bible study aids for women's groups have been published. They can be used to stimulate discussion and learning. Furthermore, besides education, these groups provide the intangible elements that are therapeutic in any group process. It provides the participants with a sense of support and mutual validation for shared feelings and experiences. The group process removes the sense of isolation and provides an extended family of adult members, mutually caring for each other. Weekly consistent meetings also provide a needed sense of structure to the week that is necessary to combat the often frenzied nature of raising young children. Ideally, these groups should be coordinated by someone who is trained or sensitive to the needs of young mothers. The leader should make an effort to provide consistency in meeting. This is often difficult to do when the demands of a young mother's life may make it impossible for her consistent attendance. The pragmatic matter of child care should be arranged so that mothers can have a much needed and possibly rare opportunity to participate in adult conversation and stimulation.

Many secular support groups have been established in various communities throughout the country. Women with postpartum depression discover that they are not alone as they learn more about their condition. When needed, church groups can borrow from the information and experiences offered by these postpartum depression support groups. Refer to the organization Depression After Delivery in the resource section of this chapter to obtain more information about support groups. Women who have recovered from postpartum depression provide strong encouragement to new mothers. The groups can be easily established in the church setting. Women's fellowships or group meetings for young mothers can address many of the issues which affect new mothers. These groups can provide emotional and spiritual support.

Support the father and the family. The family members do suffer when a woman develops postpartum depression. The father needs support, both practical help and emotional comfort, while he attends to the multiple new demands required of him. The church can offer help in many of these matters whether it be helping with overwhelming household chores, cooking, etc.

As depicted in our illustration, postpartum depression leaves a new father very confused. Having a baby is usually anticipated with much joy, and when quite the opposite occurs, the father may not be able to discern the problem. Appropriate help and counseling from the minister or other church members can mobilize the father into getting the needed professional help for his wife.

If there are other siblings in the home, the church can help by attending to their needs. Often the care of siblings can be overlooked when a mother has postpartum depression, and church members can assist where there are temporary lapses in caring for siblings.

RESOURCES

Depression After Delivery (D.A.D.)
P.O. Box 278
Belle Mead, NJ 08502
(215) 295-3994
(800) 944-4PPD

Depression After Delivery is an organization that provides information, support, education, and referrals for those suffering from postpartum depression.

* * *

Focus on the Family Program
Colorado Springs, CO 80995
(719) 531-3400 Ext. 2700

* * *

American Psychiatric Association
Division of Public Affairs
Department MM99
1400 K Street NW
Washington DC 20005
(888) 357-7924

* * *

National Depressive and Manic-Depressive Association
730 North Franklin Street
Suite 501
Chicago, IL 60610
(800) 826-3632

This organization provides educational materials regarding depression and manic-depressive disorder.

Chapter 8

Monthly Worries: PMS

Iris is a twenty-eight-year-old woman who is one of the choir members in a church. She is usually cheerful, friendly, and enjoys singing very much. The people who know her find that while she appears very contented, she sometimes seems quite stressed, tired, and nervous. Her friendly manner is replaced by withdrawal and a lack of energy. One day in choir, after the conductor remarked that she looked tired, she snapped at him and yelled, "If you had to worry about what I had to today, you'd be tired too!"

Iris apologized for her abruptness and appeared to be quite agitated. She later told a friend in the choir that lately she had been feeling irritable and anxious each month. In addition, she always had trouble with being overweight, but recently she noticed that none of her clothes fit. Her feet and fingers were swollen, and she just felt miserable.

At the next rehearsal, she was her usual cheerful self. She and her friend were both excitedly talking about the upcoming performance of Handel's *Messiah* for the special Christmas service, and they have both been given challenging solos. They planned to get together and rehearse their parts on a weekly basis. Even though it was hard work, over the weeks that followed, Iris made great progress on the solo, and both she and her friend saw that Iris was gifted with a special talent. In fact, the entire choir was at the height of perfection with just two weeks left to the performance. All the choir members were thankful and joyful at being able to serve God in song, including Iris. Two days later, the phone rang, and Iris was on the line crying, telling her friend that she felt she could not sing in the upcoming performance. She wanted to know whether her friend could take her place.

DISCUSSION

Premenstrual syndrome (PMS) has been defined in many ways and is used to describe the mood, behavioral, and physical symptoms that occur in some women during the week prior to menstruation. This phase is called the "late luteal phase." During this time many women may experience symptoms ranging from a single mild symptom to having a collection of symptoms severe enough to cause problems in function, or their PMS may interfere with their social relationships. These symptoms should end just after the onset of the menstrual period.

To improve our knowledge of PMS, the *Diagnostic and Statistical Manual of Mental Disorders,* Fourth Edition, has proposed the following definition for the study of PMS, which is called "Premenstrual Dysphoric Disorder."[1] The criteria states that:

1. A woman should experience premenstrual symptoms nearly every cycle for the past year.
2. She must experience at least 5 of the following symptoms including one from the first four:
3. Depressed mood (sad, self-deprecating thoughts)
4. Anxiety (feeling tense)
5. Mood lability—This refers to rapid changes in mood from sad to happy in a short period of time.
6. Irritability
7. Change in appetite
8. Sleep disturbance
9. Tiredness
10. Withdrawal from social activities

11. Various physical complaints including bloating, headache, or worsening of existing medical problems.
12. These symptoms are severe enough to impair a woman's ability to function and should be distinguished from other psychiatric conditions such as clinical depression, anxiety disorders, or other mood disorders. The diagnosis has to be confirmed by two months of testing using a daily rating form.

(Reprinted with permission from the *Diagnostic and Statistical Manual of Mental Disorders,* Fourth Edition. Copyright 1994 American Psychiatric Association)

The majority of women experience isolated symptoms or mild symptoms but do not fit this criteria. Only a small percentage of women actually have premenstrual dysphoric disorder. Because of the controversy surrounding its definition, it is important for women to seek help in identifying whether they have another psychiatric condition that can be treated.

Premenstrual symptoms can also be addressed in a number of other ways, including lifestyle changes. Women will benefit from proper exercise. For some reason exercise increases a body chemical called "endorphin" which improves a person's sense of well-being. Although it may not cure PMS, it certainly will help the mood changes that some women experience during the premenstrual week. Proper nutrition is also important. Decreasing dietary intake of salt will help cut down on fluid retention and the symptom of bloating. Caffeine restriction may also be helpful in reducing breast discomfort. Managing stress in the premenstrual week is an important strategy. For example, if a woman has some control over her schedule, she can choose to perform more stressful tasks at a time other than the premenstrual week. The effectiveness of vitamin supplementation is controversial. However women do utilize them. Dr. Mary Jane Minkin, a gynecologist with the Yale University Medical College, writes that she has recommended vitamin B6, vitamin E, and a health supplement called "evening primrose oil" for PMS. She has found that they have been helpful in many cases.[2] Other treatments include various hormonal regimens that should be discussed with a gynecologist. Diuretics are sometimes used to treat bloating, but this should be monitored by a physician to prevent disturbing the body's potassium supply. Finally, there are increasing reports that the newer antidepressants, called selective serotonin reuptake inhibitors (SSRIs) such as Prozac (fluoxetine) and Zoloft (sertraline) may be effective in the treatment of some women with premenstrual syndromes. Dr. Anna L. Stout, of Duke University Medical Center, reported on a research project involving twelve academic centers that studied 234 women with the diagnosis of premenstrual dysphoric disorder. The study showed that Zoloft (sertraline) was significantly more effective than a placebo in the treatment of these women.[3] Women with a family history or a previous personal history of depression with PMS should consider obtaining a psychiatric evaluation for depression and the possible use of an antidepressant.

Treatment of underlying psychiatric conditions is also important to relieve some symptoms that are exacerbated in the premenstrual period. For example, if a woman suffers from panic disorder and she is more anxious premenstrually, she may attribute her panic attacks to PMS. It is also important that clinical depression be distinguished from PMS. If a woman's PMS lasts for several weeks per month, it is not PMS but more likely to be something else such as depression. It is important to discern this as there are effective treatments for depression. A proper evaluation by a gynecologist or a psychiatrist who specializes in the areas of PMS will provide a diagnosis. A well-integrated approach including psychiatric and gynecologic care as well as lifestyle improvements are recommended.

Iris's case is typical of many women who have premenstrual symptoms. She experiences abdominal bloating such that her clothes do not fit. She generally seems well but then surprisingly becomes irritable, snappy, tired, anxious about not just her routine but about a singing engagement that she has clearly mastered. The anxiety in the premenstrual week has changed her perception of her abilities by making her anxious. Iris does bring her complaints to her gynecologist and finds that she has a normal gynecologic examination. She then sees the psychiatrist referred by her gynecologist, and soon a diagnosis is made. Iris has premenstrual dysphoric disorder. In the past, she has had clinical depressions that have never been treated. Medication and counseling are provided. She begins to learn more about PMS and makes the necessary changes in her life. It should not be surprising that she goes on to sing the Hallelujah chorus with confidence and excellence. Congratulations to this and the many other Marthas in the church.

HOW THE CHURCH CAN HELP

The church community can offer vital assistance in the lifestyle changes that work for women who suffer from premenstrual syndrome. General rules of good health such as exercise, proper nutrition, and limitation of the use of agents such as alcohol, caffeine, salt, and fat can be incorporated into a program designed for women. The program can take the form of a regular exercise group meeting at the church integrated with educational workshops. The underlying philosophy of the group should be taking care of the body as a form of proper stewardship of the body that God has given each woman. Hence, biblical study and support can be offered to motivate the members to continue in the proper care of their bodies. When such a program is effective, it offers women mutual support, accountability to one another in maintaining disciplined exercise, and the opportunity to share health information.

An example of this type of program is the "Body and Soul Ministries." They have developed an exercise program that can be utilized in any church setting. It is designed to work for the Christian woman. The program has established numerous expertly designed aerobics classes throughout different Christian settings in the country. They have developed a training program and materials including videotapes, CDs, and manuals that provide ongoing instruction for the exercise class and its leader. Combining the scriptural teaching which is drawn from the music that is used for the exercises as well as from the Bible, the Body and Soul Ministry has served to combine a program of good physical as well as spiritual health. Advocates of the program have testified to its positive effect on physical well-being and mood, as well as on the management of chronic illnesses such as diabetes mellitus. Certainly it can benefit those women suffering from PMS. For more information, please refer to the resource section of this chapter.

Health education is an important tool and can be disseminated in the church setting whether it is done in women's groups or provided in publications. In the field of PMS, there are many different treatments that have been offered as well as new developments in both the self-help and medical arenas.

For the individual woman who is suffering from PMS or knows someone who is, try to learn as much as you can about PMS, depression and anxiety disorders. You can obtain information from books, magazines, people in the medical or mental health field and even from patients who have been successfully treated. Being well informed is one way you can be of help to the women in your church.

Encouragement is a tool for handling PMS. Because of the cyclical nature of PMS, women can quickly appreciate that there are days in the month when anxiety, depression, or physical tension can affect perceptions of their own performance and life in general. They also can recognize that these conditions resolve with the onset of menses. It is helpful for women to remind one another that the mood symptoms will abate and that they will return to normal. When possible, they can assist one another by sharing responsibilities. Most important, the psychological support offered by women to other women is invaluable.

Caring church members can help women who are debilitated by their premenstrual symptoms by suggesting professional or medical intervention. It is useful to know the differences between professional resources when you refer someone for help. Gynecologists are medical doctors who are expert in the biology of the female reproductive system and therefore can evaluate whether there is anything wrong physically. A psychiatrist is also a medical doctor who can determine whether mood changes that may be attributed to PMS, might be the result of a treatable mental condition such as depression or anxiety disorder. They can provide medication as well as psychotherapy (talk therapy) and counseling. Psychologists, social workers, and psychotherapists generally are trained to provide different forms of counseling and talk therapy. They do not prescribe medications but some may work in collaboration with a psychiatrist when medication is needed.

Sufferers play a unique role in helping other sufferers. This is described in the following Scripture passage:

> Praise be to the God and Father of our Lord Jesus Christ, the Father of compassion and the God of all comfort, who comforts us in all our troubles, so that we can comfort those in any trouble with the comfort we ourselves have received from God.[4]

Individuals who have suffered and recovered from a mental illness represent a great resource of information, experience, and testimony to those who are afflicted for the first time. The Christian who has had experience with depression, anxiety disorders, or premenstrual dysphoric disorder has learned many lessons and facts about the process of recovery that would be of vital encouragement to those who need to travel a similar route. These lessons can be communicated to facilitate the journey. For example, a Christian who has recovered from mental illness can tell the sufferer that he or she can view treatment and/or medication as tools that God has provided for the healing of the sufferer. He can teach the sufferer that having a mental illness is not a result of sin as many are apt to believe but rather like all disease processes, the result of living in an imperfect world with imperfect bodies. Where treatments exist, one should take advantage of these and Christians can thank God for them. Christian sufferers who have recovered can gently guide those through the maze of treatment seeking. And most important, they provide the comfort to those who are suffering by communicating to them that they are not alone, that these problems do occur among Christians and that they are the evidence that it can be overcome.

Although the ability of Christian sufferers to help other sufferers is valid and important across all mental illnesses, why include it in a chapter on PMS? There are two reasons. First, PMS is a uniquely woman's issue at least from a biological perspective. Many women feel comfortable in talking to and confiding with other women about health problems and perhaps to a lesser degree about mental health issues. Whether it is in a group forum in church or in the many quiet conversations between two women, many mental health symptoms and difficult to talk about concerns are shared. In recent years, there has been increasing ease for women to talk openly about PMS. Partly through improved health education in the media and partly because it seems so widespread, women do not find it as stigmatizing to talk about their monthly symptoms. In fact, many women will readily go to the doctor to get help for PMS much more so than seeking the same consultation for depression or another mental illness. Ironically, because the symptoms of PMS are similar to psychiatric conditions, these women discover that what they really have is a clinical depression or an anxiety disorder. If this occurs, and they are directed to the appropriate treatment, they will benefit from receiving the proper diagnosis. This leads to the second reason why the notion of PMS represents an opportunity for recovered sufferers to help others.

Premenstrual syndrome is often the diagnosis women make about themselves when what they really have may be an exacerbation of psychiatric or medical conditions including endometriosis, pelvic inflammatory disease, clinical depression, eating disorders, or anxiety disorders. A physician can make the appropriate determination. Some evidence supports the fact that a subgroup of women who have premenstrual dysphoric disorder have a condition that resembles a clinical depression period. This group of women responds well to antidepressants. In any case, women choose to use PMS as a description for symptoms of other conditions that are exacerbated premenstrually. Since this occurs, it requires a thorough physician to ensure proper diagnosis.

It also requires thoughtful friends and caring family to help uncover these mistakes and direct women to the proper help. Women who have labeled their symptoms as PMS and then find that they have depression or anxiety disorders can help educate their peers with sensitivity. That is to say, they understand the need to label symptoms with the neutral title of PMS while at the same time be able to help look for the real underlying condition. They have learned to discern when PMS is *not* PMS. For example, PMS is not PMS when the woman notes symptoms for more than two weeks out of every month. This is too long a period to be truly premenstrual. It is not PMS when her only "good week" is not that good relative to her usual self. In other words, if she is depressed or anxious all month but much more so during the week prior to menses, this does not support the diagnosis of PMS. It is not PMS when a woman is totally incapacitated or suicidal. It is far better to look for other treatable causes of these conditions. Technically, it cannot be called PMS if the woman is taking oral contraceptives simply because contraceptives prevent ovulation and the hormonal events that create a normal menstrual cycle. While a doctor would make the definitive diagnosis after evaluation, women who have suffered from these conditions can help their peers sort out their symptoms just by sharing information.

The process in which a recovered sufferer helps another whether it be in the area of premenstrual dysphoric disorder or other psychiatric illnesses, requires a certain amount of self-revelation. Clearly, when it is done in a timely and appropriate manner, it is helpful. Support groups for the various illnesses have testified to the benefit of mutual support, health education, self-help, and professional attention. This type of support can occur on an individual level from one sufferer to another. However, this is not an argument for total self-revelation without discrimination. There are advantages and drawbacks which again relate to the stigmatization that comes from societal ignorance to those who have a mental illness. There are also individual circumstances and factors to consider. Hence, self-revelation must be an individualized decision and ultimately a choice. When one person reveals information about himself or herself to help another, ideally this should be met with respect and gratitude. The person has risked his or her privacy and potential stigmatization to help educate another. In the best scenario, there would be mutual benefit.

In concluding this chapter and book, clinical experience and private testimonies are proof that these scenarios are happening all the time in various church communities. People privately help one another through life experiences that often are not talked about in public. This should be applauded. It is the intention of this book to augment and foster this process for the sake of our Marthas.

RESOURCES

Premenstrual Syndrome Program
University of Pennsylvania Medical Center
Department of Obstetrics and Gynecology
Philadelphia, PA 19104-4283

* * *

Dr. Anna Stout
Duke University Medical Center
Women's Behavioral Health Program
Box 3263
Durham, NC 27710

* * *

North American Society for Psychosocial Obstetrics
    and Gynecology (NASPOG)
409 12th Street SW
Washington, DC 20024-2188
(202) 863-1648
www.NASPOG.org

* * *

Body and Soul Ministries
P.O. Box 2288
Germantown, MD 20875
(301) 258-1018
www.bodyandsoul.org

Appendix

The Final Word

All of us struggle with many worries including concerns about our health, our jobs, our families, and our future. Some of these worries may represent responses to genuine stressful life situations and other worries may be due, as we have learned, to psychological or medical conditions. Hopefully, this book has provided information, insight, and direction regarding anxiety disorders that will broaden our understanding of how Christians worry.

In any event, why do we worry when the Bible tells us not to have any anxiety in anything? If worrying about the body and daily bread cannot add one iota to life, why do we do it? We know that God can adorn the lilies and feed the sparrows. Therefore, He can also attend to our personal concerns.

What are your worries both past and present? How have you coped with your fears and what role has God taken? As for your future concerns, God's Word can also play a role. It is a good resource to help you with anxiety. As a final word, the following Scripture verses are recommended.[1] Like Mary, sit at Jesus's feet and meditate on the Word of God.

> Isaiah 41:10: So do not fear, for I am with you; do not be dismayed, for I am your God. I will strengthen you and help you; I will uphold you with my righteous right hand.

The promise of God's strength, assistance and support along the turbulent road of life is reason to remain calm and unperplexed. People do well in hard times, and may even thrive, with adequate support. But when that help comes from an Almighty source, there is greater reason for tranquility instead of fear.

> Proverbs 1:33: . . . but whoever listens to me [Wisdom] will live in safety and be at ease, without fear of harm.

Proverbial wisdom, as described here, is God's instruction. It provides a foundation as well as guidelines for being at ease and safe. Despite any onslaught of real life stress or emotional turbulence caused by anxious thinking, the essential truth for the believing Christian is that there is "no fear of harm."

> Psalm 23:4: Even though I walk through the valley of the shadow of death, I will fear no evil, for you are with me; your rod and your staff, they comfort me.

Many patients with anxiety disorders have an overwhelming fear and preoccupation with having or developing a serious medical illness such as cancer or a heart attack. What makes this a serious illness is that the end result is death. One does not need to have an anxiety disorder to fear death. In our strongly thanophobic society, death is a force to be conquered, grieved, processed, denied, avoided, and if all else fails, delayed. Religious faith offers another solution. This Scripture verse, spoken at many funerals, indicates that death or "walking in the valley of the shadow of death" need not to be feared in the presence of a God who comforts. Death can bring on sadness and a sense of loss or separation but it does not need to be feared. The strength of this concept lies in the person's ability to incorporate it into his or her belief system. Although it may be futile to insist that a person accept this belief while in the throes of a panic attack or hypochondriacal crisis, this idea can be comprehended in the appropriate time. Simply observe its usefulness during funeral services. Many times, the verse is also uttered in prayer during a time of imminent peril, the foxhole experiences of a person's life.

Psalm 37:23: If the Lord delights in a man's way, he makes his steps firm.

An enormous amount of stress is generated by doing what is illegal, immoral, or just plain wrong. In contrast, if one stays within the confines of moral or civil law and similarly if a Christian walks in a path consistent with God's way, he or she does not bring upon himself or herself the stress and anxiety that accompanies wrongdoing. In fact, the Lord makes one's "steps firm." Consider this an important principle of stress management and prevention.

> Mark 6:45-51: "Immediately Jesus made his disciples get into the boat and go on ahead of him to Bethsaida, while he dismissed the crowd. After leaving them, he went up on a mountainside to pray. When evening came, the boat was in the middle of the lake, and he was alone on land. He saw the disciples straining at the oars, because the wind was against them. About the fourth watch of the night he went out to them, walking on the lake. He was about to pass by them, but when they saw him walking on the lake, they thought he was a ghost. They cried out, because they all saw him and were terrified.
>
> Immediately he spoke to them and said, "Take courage! It is I. Don't be afraid." Then he climbed into the boat with them, and the wind died down. They were completely amazed.

The Bible offers us many snapshots of human fear and anxiety and God's response to them. Jesus' reassurance to the disciples in the midst of rough water is, "Take courage! It is I." Jesus being powerfully God yet empathetically human is a means of true comfort and amazement to his frightened disciples. This image is by no means lost to today's Christians.

In the practical application of this image to the worrying Christian today, consider the use of "visualization techniques" as part of relaxation exercises. This technique involves having the person mentally visualize a calming, restful scene of his or her own choice. Common examples would be a sunny beach scene, a warm meadow on a spring day, or a gentle waterfall, generally chosen from the individual's repertoire of experiences. Christians can and often do choose scenes from a biblical passage that conveys a sense of calm. The picture of Jesus' strong and comforting presence as portrayed in this passage can be utilized in visualization techniques to enhance relaxation. Another biblical image involves picturing oneself as a tree planted by a stream of water, which is a metaphor for a man who delights and meditates on God's Word. Calming biblical images are highly individualized and should be derived from one's personal experience. When discovered, they can be incorporated into a program of relaxation.

> Psalm 112:1-10: Praise the Lord. Blessed is the man who fears the Lord, who finds great delight in his commands. His children will be mighty in the land; the generation of the upright will be blessed. Wealth and riches are in his house, and his righteousness endures forever. Even in darkness light dawns for the upright, for the gracious and compassionate and righteous man. Good will come to him who is generous and lends freely, who conducts his affairs with justice. Surely he will never be shaken; a righteous man will be remembered forever. He will have no fear of bad news; his heart is steadfast, trusting in the Lord. His heart is secure, he will have no fear; in the end he will look in triumph on his foes. He has scattered abroad his gifts to the poor, his righteousness endures forever; his horn will be lifted high in honor. The wicked man will see and be vexed, he will gnash his teeth and waste away; the longings of the wicked will come to nothing.

Holy fear results in no fear. That is the essence of this passage from the psalmist. The blessings that ensue from fearing the Lord are manifold. They comprise the areas of life that worry many people today—children, wealth, time, security, and honor. Reverential fear of the Lord, combined with obedience to God's commands, compassion, and generosity, form the basis for a sanctified life.

> John 16:33: I have told you these things, so that in me you may have peace. In this world you will have trouble. But take heart! I have overcome the world.

This verse is Jesus' promise to his disciples. His realistic foretelling of the troubles that the world will bring is countered by the assurance that He has guaranteed their peace. In the same way, Christians need to understand that realistically they will experience stressors in their lives, but they can turn their thoughts to God who has overcome the world and maintain inner tranquility. Even more important is this message for the person prone to anxiety who generally appraises every situation, good or bad, as having potential for catastrophe. This person should employ this biblical truth to restructure automatic, negativistic, anxiety-provoking thoughts to those that are more realistic, positive, and pacifying.

> Romans 8:15-16: For you did not receive a spirit that makes you a slave again to fear, but you received the Spirit of sonship. And by him we cry, "Abba, Father." The Spirit himself testifies with our spirit that we are God's children.

Believing that we are sons of God through Christ rather than slaves to sin is the crux of the Christian faith. Because of this, we are expected to master fear because of the special standing of sonship to Abba, Father. Our thoughts should be conformed to this new relationship. Hence, anxious people need to focus on God's parental love and not the judgment of a harsh slavedriver.

> Philippians 4:6-9: Do not be anxious about anything, but in everything, by prayer and petition, with thanksgiving, pre-

sent your requests to God. And the peace of God, which transcends all understanding, will guard your hearts and your minds in Christ Jesus.

Finally, brothers, whatever is true, whatever is noble, whatever is right, whatever is pure, whatever is lovely, whatever is admirable—if anything is excellent or praise-worthy—think about such things. Whatever you have learned or received or heard from me, or seen in me—put it into practice. And the God of peace will be with you.

This is one of the most popular passages in Scripture address-ing anxiety, and for good reason. It provides a series of steps to take when one is anxious:

1. Halt the anxious thinking.
2. Turn your attention to God.
3. Pray to Him regarding the stressor.
4. Thank Him for all you can.
5. Distract yourself from the anxiety.
6. Turn your thoughts to that which is noble, pure, lovely, and admirable.

It is beneficial to meditate on the truth of these verses. If you take the steps derived from the passage you will influence the mental processes generating anxiety. This is biblically directed cognitive restructuring at its finest.

2 Thessalonians 3:3: But the Lord is faithful, and he will strengthen and protect you from the evil one.

The doctrine of the devil or the "evil one" is totally in the theological realm and has no real counterpart in the psychologi-cal world. Granted, attempts are made at psychologic explana-tions for the entity of the devil or evil in general but as a real concrete person, only fundamental Christian faith provides for its definition. Given that Christians believe in satanic oppression as one cause of stress and anxiety, it would be pragmatic and even therapeutic to offer biblical reassurance of protection from the evil one. For many Christians, knowing that the devil may be behind much of their fear and anxiety gives them enough impetus to persevere and function despite great fear or obstacle. Somehow the very realization that they are experiencing fear and affliction by the evil one because they are on the right track of living a holy life renders some Christians ready to meet the challenge. Furthermore when there is biblical support for God's power and might over the evil one and His ability to protect, many Christians take great comfort even while struggling. This doctrine remains a theologically based tool which plays a vital role in the church's work against anxiety.

> Hebrews 13:6: So we say with confidence, "The Lord is my helper; I will not be afraid. What can man do to me?"

When anxious patients speak of the dread they anticipate in a given situation, I often ask them, "Tell me, what do you think is the worst that can happen?" When they actually go through the process, they realize that the worst is really not so bad. It certainly did not merit the kind of fear they were experiencing. The rhetorical query, "What can man do to me?" is analogous to my line of questioning. And more important, Christians can have the advantage of acknowledging, "The Lord is my helper."

> Psalm 27:1-14: The Lord is my light and my salvation— whom shall I fear? The Lord is the stronghold of my life— of whom shall I be afraid? When evil men advance against me to devour my flesh, when my enemies and my foes attack me, they will stumble and fall. Though an army besiege me, my heart will not fear; though war break out against me, even then will I be confident. One thing I ask of the Lord, this is what I seek: that I may dwell in the house of

the Lord all the days of my life, to gaze upon the beauty of the Lord and to seek him in his temple. For in the day of trouble he will keep me safe in his dwelling; he will hide me in the shelter of his tabernacle and set me high upon a rock. Then my head will be exalted above the enemies who surround me; at his tabernacle will I sacrifice with shouts of joy; I will sing and make music to the Lord. Hear my voice when I call, O Lord; be merciful to me and answer me. My heart says of you, "Seek his face!" Your face, Lord, I will seek. Do not hide your face from me, do not turn your servant away in anger; you have been my helper. Do not reject me or forsake me, O God my Savior. Though my father and mother forsake me, the Lord will receive me. Teach me your way, O Lord; lead me in a straight path because of my oppressors. Do not turn me over to the desire of my foes, for false witnesses rise up against me, breathing out violence. I am still confident of this: I will see the goodness of the Lord in the land of the living. Wait for the Lord; be strong and take heart and wait for the Lord.

This prayer juxtaposes two combating themes. One is modified by words such as *light, salvation, stronghold, confident, joy, singing, goodness, taking heart,* and *waiting for the Lord.* This is compared to the opposing thoughts that are expressed in the words *fear, stumble, war, enemies, oppressors,* and *breathing violence.* This prayer expresses the cognitive struggle of a man trying to use his thoughts to reduce the anxiety generated by a forceful onslaught of fear producing images. This anxiety is most likely situationally induced. The cognitive battle and its success is based on the belief in the sovereignty of God. This prayer is illustrative of the cognitive processes of many Christians undergoing stress. For many, it represents a powerful, theologically generated coping skill.

Psalm 56:3-4: When I am afraid, I will trust in you. In God, whose word I praise, in God I trust; I will not be afraid. What can mortal man do to me?

The sequence of thoughts in this passage is signaled by the emotion of fear. The response of the believer is to confront fear by acknowledgement of trust in God and His Word. This acknowledgement results in the shift to the new state, "I will not be afraid." This is the essence of Christian cognitive restructuring, that is the change in mood rendered by adopting into one's cognition, realities, in this case spiritual, for the purpose of altering the mood state. Once the quelling of the fear is achieved, it is further bolstered by the rhetorical question, "What can mortal man do to me?" For the believer, this reflection underscores the notion that nothing mortal man can inflict upon the believer is beyond the scope of God's trustworthy care and protection.

Proverbs 12:25: An anxious heart weighs a man down, but a kind word cheers him up.

When caring for the "Marthas" in your church, do not underestimate the power of an encouraging word. Even if the comfort is temporary, it provides a moment of relief by cheering the heart. This is supported by biblical wisdom and can be done quite well by anybody who is willing.

Jeremiah 29:11-13: "For I know the plans I have for you," declares the Lord, "plans to prosper you and not to harm you, plans to give you hope and a future. Then you will call upon me and come and pray to me, and I will listen to you. You will seek me and find me when you seek me with all your heart."

The future is often plagued with misgivings and worry for anxious people. Circumstantial changes are often unsettling and anxiety provoking. This verse indicates that one can counter the worries about potential problems by acknowledging in faith that God has plans to prosper and not to harm. One can forebear changes and crises by keeping a positive focus on the future based on this verse.

> Matthew 10:29-31: Are not two sparrows sold for a penny? Yet not one of them will fall to the ground apart from the will of your Father. And even the very hairs of your head are all numbered. So don't be afraid; you are worth more than many sparrows.

The anxious Christian needs to know that God is in control even though he or she feels out of control from worry. The Christian also needs to understand his or her great personal worth to a God who will care for him or her. Understanding these biblical precepts will offset the concerns that plague the individual and temper the emotion of anxiety.

> Matthew 14:22-27: Immediately Jesus made the disciples get into the boat and go on ahead of him to the other side, while he dismissed the crowd. After he had dismissed them, he went up on a mountainside by himself to pray. When evening came, he was there alone, but the boat was already a considerable distance from land, buffeted by the waves because the wind was against it.
>
> During the fourth watch of the night Jesus went out to them, walking on the lake. When the disciples saw him walking on the lake, they were terrified. "It's a ghost," they said, and cried out in fear.
>
> But Jesus immediately said to them: "Take courage! It is I. Don't be afraid."

The disciples were afraid when they saw Jesus walking on the water toward them and concluded, "It's a ghost." Their fear, understandingly, heightened by the buffeting waves, was in response to a misperception. This was not a ghost but their friend and teacher. Anxiety often occurs in response to misperceptions and therefore it is always important to evaluate any situation carefully before making anxiety-provoking conclusions.

> 2 Corinthians 1:3-4: Praise be to the God and Father of our Lord Jesus Christ, the Father of compassion and the God of all comfort, who comforts us in all our troubles, so that we can comfort those in any trouble with the comfort we ourselves have received from God.

The comforting nature of God is the foundation for the comfort that Christians give to each other. This becomes the basis for the support that Christians can give to one another. The end of each chapter in this book provides instruction as to how Christians can help those who are afflicted with anxiety disorders. The recommendations are offered with the belief as stated in this verse that Christians can and do help comfort one another with the help of God.

> 2 Timothy 1:7: For God did not give us a spirit of timidity, but a spirit of power, of love and of self-discipline.

In working with phobic patients, I have recognized that those who succeed in mastering their fears have two main strengths. One is a strong motivation and the other is the self-discipline and perseverance it takes to endure anxious moments to practice exposing themselves to a feared stimulus. We are given power, love, and self-discipline that can be employed along with some professional training to overcome anxiety.

> 1 Chronicles 28:20: David also said to Solomon his son, "Be strong and courageous, and do the work. Do not be afraid or discouraged, for the Lord God, my God, is with

you. He will not fail you or forsake you until all the work
for the service of the temple of the Lord is finished."

Lamentations 3:22-23: Because of the Lord's great love we
are not consumed, for his compassions never fail. They are
new every morning; great is your faithfulness.

People speak in terms of being "consumed" with worry, anxiety,
or doubt. Obsessions can be viewed as a form of mental consumption. And despite the power of strong human emotion, Christians
are anchored by this promise: they are not consumed. That is,
though they feel consumed, in fact, they are not consumed. The
renewal of God's compassion as a source of new hope each morning provides faithful reassurance despite difficult times.

Hebrews 4:14-16: Therefore, since we have a great high
priest who has gone through the heavens, Jesus the Son of
God, let us hold firmly to the faith we profess. For we do
not have a high priest who is unable to sympathize with our
weaknesses, but we have one who has been tempted in
every way, just as we are—yet was without sin. Let us then
approach the throne of grace with confidence, so that we
may receive mercy and find grace to help us in our time of
need.

Having a merciful and sympathetic "high priest," who can
empathize with our anxiety provides us with the confidence to
persevere. It is much like having a "listening ear" who is also a
strong advocate and source of help. Because of this, anxious
Christians do not have to live in self-condemnation for their
anxiety. They only need to focus their efforts in overcoming it.

2 Corinthians 7:5-7: For when we came into Macedonia,
this body of ours had no rest, but we were harassed at every
turn—conflicts on the outside, fears within. But God, who

comforts the downcast, comforted us by the coming of Titus, and not only by his coming but also by the comfort you had given him. He told us about your longing for me, your deep sorrow, your ardent concern for me, so that my joy was greater than ever.

The therapeutic value of Christian caring and concern is one of the major legacies of the church. Paul, at this point in his ministry, would be a good candidate for modern day stress management seminars. His body had no rest; he was struggling with external conflicts and experiencing internal fears. He then writes about the tremendous comfort and relief at the appearance of a fellow colleague, Titus. Moreover, Paul spoke of the joy he derived from hearing about the Corinthians' sympathy, burden, and care for him. This supportive role is what the ideal church has done well throughout the centuries.

> Proverbs 3:25, 26: Have no fear of sudden disaster or of the ruin that overtakes the wicked, for the Lord will be your confidence and will keep your foot from being snared.

The unpredictability and damaging consequences of sudden disaster frightens many. People take multiple precautions for all kinds of catastrophe, but there is no real guarantee that the measures they take will work. One need not live in fear of sudden disaster. That sort of life is emotionally crippling and unnecessary. For Christians, this verse reminds them of the security they have in God.

> Luke 2:10-11: But the angel said to them, "Do not be afraid. I bring you good news of great joy that will be for all the people. Today in the town of David a Savior has been born to you; he is Christ the Lord."

Fear not!

Notes

Introduction

1. International Bible Society, *Holy Bible: New International Version.* (Grand Rapids, MI: Zondervan, 1984), Luke 10:38-42.
2. International Bible Society, 1984, Philippians 4:6.

Chapter 1

1. International Bible Society, *Holy Bible: New International Version.* (Grand Rapids, MI: Zondervan, 1984), Proverbs 24:26.
2. American Psychiatric Association, *Diagnostic and Statistical Manual of Mental Disorders,* Fourth Edition. (Washington DC: American Psychiatric Press, 1994), p. 419.
3. International Bible Society, 1984, John 3:16.
4. International Bible Society, 1984, 1 John 1:9.
5. Personal communication from Dr. Bruce Ballard, Associate Dean of Medical Students at Cornell University Medical College.

Chapter 2

1. Jerrold R. Rosenbaum, Treatment of panic disorder: The state of the art. *Journal of Clinical Psychiatry,* 1997:58 (supplement #2) p. 3.
2. International Bible Society, *Holy Bible: New International Version.* (Grand Rapids, MI: Zondervan, 1984), Jeremiah 29:11.
3. *Holy Bible, King James Version* (Nashville, TN: Thomas Nelson Publishers, 1984), Psalm 115:11.
4. *Holy Bible, King James Version* (Nashville, TN: Thomas Nelson Publishers, 1984), 2 Timothy 1:7.

Chapter 3

1. Information obtained with permission from Sister Sheila Lyne. This is obtained from her address to the North American Society for Psychosocial Obstetrics and Gynecology held in Chicago, February 13, 1997.

2. International Bible Society, *Holy Bible: New International Version.* (Grand Rapids, MI: Zondervan, 1984), Psalm 10:8-11.

Chapter 4

1. International Bible Society, *Holy Bible: New International Version.* (Grand Rapids, MI: Zondervan, 1984), Proverbs 19:20, Proverbs 20:18.

Chapter 5

1. International Bible Society, *Holy Bible: New International Version.* (Grand Rapids, MI: Zondervan, 1984), 1 Corinthians 12:25-27.

Chapter 6

1. International Bible Society, *Holy Bible: New International Version.* (Grand Rapids, MI: Zondervan, 1984), 2 Corinthians 7:5-6.
2. International Bible Society, 1984, Philippians 4:6-7.

Chapter 7

1. American Psychiatric Association, *Diagnostic and Statistical Manual of Mental Disorders,* Fourth Edition. (Washington, DC: American Psychiatric Press, 1994), p. 341.
2. International Bible Society, *Holy Bible: New International Version.* (Grand Rapids, MI: Zondervan, 1984), Psalm 88:1-18.
3. Quote from American Psychiatric Association's literature for National Depression Screening Day, 1994.
4. Sheldon H. Cherry and Irwin R. Merkatz (editors), *Complications of Pregnancy: Medical, Surgical, Gynecologic, Psychosocial, and Perinatal* (Baltimore: Williams and Wilkins, 1991), p. 227.

Chapter 8

1. American Psychiatric Association, *Diagnostic and Statistical Manual of Mental Disorders,* Fourth Edition. (Washington, DC: American Psychiatric Press, 1994), p. 715.
2. Mary Jane Minkin and Carol Wright, *What Every Woman Needs to Know About Menopause* (New Haven: Yale University Press, 1996), pp. 38-39.
3. K. A. Yonkers, U. Halgreich, E. Freeman, C. Brown, J. Endicott, E. Frank, B. Parry, T. Pearlstein, S. Severino, A. Stout, S. Stone, and W. Harrison, Symptomatic

improvement of premenstrual dysphoria with sertraline treatment: A randomized control trial. *Journal of American Medical Association,* 1997:278(12), pp. 983-988.

4. International Bible Society, *Holy Bible: New International Version.* (Grand Rapids, MI: Zondervan, 1984), 2 Corinthians 1:3,4.

Appendix

1. All verses cited are quoted from International Bible Society, *Holy Bible: New International Version.* (Grand Rapids, MI: Zondervan, 1984).

Bibliography

American Psychiatric Association, *Diagnostic and Statistical Manual of Mental Disorders,* Fourth Edition. Washington, DC: American Psychiatric Press, 1994.

American Psychological Association—Division 12. Training in and dissemination of empirically-validated psychological treatments: Report and recommendations. *The Clinical Psychologist,* Winter 1995: 48, 22-23.

Backus, W. *Telling the Truth to Troubled People.* Minneapolis: Bethany House Publishers, 1985.

Barlow, D. *Anxiety and Its Disorders.* New York: Guilford Press, 1988.

Breier, A., Charney, D.S, and Heninger, G.R. Agoraphobia with panic attacks: Development, diagnostic stability, and course of illness. *Archives of General Psychiatry,* 1986: 43, 1029-1036.

Cherry, S.H. and Merkatz, I.R. (Eds.). *Complications of Pregnancy: Medical, Surgical, Gynecologic, Psychosocial, and Perinatal.* Baltimore, MD: Williams and Wilkins, 1991.

Collins, E.P. and Landsren, B. Psychoneuroendocrine stress responses and mood as related to the menstrual cycle. *Psychosomatic Medicine,* 1985: 6, 512-527.

Holy Bible, King James Version. Nashville, TN: Thomas Nelson Publishers, 1984.

International Bible Society, *Holy Bible, New International Version.* Grand Rapids, MI: Zondervan, 1984.

Kent, C., *Tame Your Fears.* Colorado Springs, CO: Navpress, 1993.

Michels, R. (Ed.). *Psychiatry.* Philadelphia: Lippincott Co., 1988.

Minkin, M.J. and Wright, C. *What Every Woman Needs to Know About Menopause.* New Haven: Yale University Press, 1996.

Minirth, F., Meier, P., and Hawkins, D. *Worry-Free Living.* Nashville, TN: Thomas Nelson Inc., 1989.

Rosenbaum, J.R. Treatment of panic disorder: The state of the art. *Journal of Clinical Psychiatry,* 1997: 58, 3.

Rubinow, D.R. and Roy-Byrne, P. Premenstrual syndromes: Overview from a methodologic perspective. *American Journal of Psychiatry,* 1984: 141, 163-172.

Speroff, L., Glass R.H., and Kase, N.G. *Clinical Gynecologic Endocrinology and Infertility.* Baltimore, MD: Williams and Wilkins, 1989.

Van Der Molen, G.M., Merckelbach, H., and Van Den Houts, M.A. The possible relation of the menstrual cycle to susceptibility to fear acquisition. *Journal of Behavioral Therapy and Experimental Psychiatry,* 1988: 19, 127-133.

Wordworks Software Architects, *Holy Bible.* Colorado Springs, CO: Navpress, 1992.

Yonkers, K.A., Halgreich, U., Freeman, E., Brown, C., Endicott, J., Frank, E., Parry, B., Pearlstein, T., Severino, S., Stout, A., Stone, S., and Harrison, W. Symptomatic improvement of premenstrual dysphoria with sertraline treatment: A randomized control trial. *Journal of the American Medical Association,* 1997: 278(12), 983-988.

Index

Order Your Own Copy of
This Important Book for Your Personal Library!

"MARTHA, MARTHA"
How Christians Worry

_____ in hardbound at $39.95 (ISBN: 0-7890-0865-3)

_____ in softbound at $14.95 (ISBN: 0-7890-0866-1)

COST OF BOOKS_____

OUTSIDE USA/CANADA/
MEXICO: ADD 20%_____

POSTAGE & HANDLING_____
(US: $3.00 for first book & $1.25
for each additional book)
Outside US: $4.75 for first book
& $1.75 for each additional book)

SUBTOTAL_____

IN CANADA: ADD 7% GST_____

STATE TAX_____
(NY, OH & MN residents, please
add appropriate local sales tax)

FINAL TOTAL_____
(If paying in Canadian funds,
convert using the current
exchange rate. UNESCO
coupons welcome.)

Prices in US dollars and subject to change without notice.

☐ **BILL ME LATER:** ($5 service charge will be added)
(Bill-me option is good on US/Canada/Mexico orders only;
not good to jobbers, wholesalers, or subscription agencies.)

☐ Check here if billing address is different from
shipping address and attach purchase order and
billing address information.

Signature_____

☐ **PAYMENT ENCLOSED: $**_____

☐ **PLEASE CHARGE TO MY CREDIT CARD.**

☐ Visa ☐ MasterCard ☐ AmEx ☐ Discover
☐ Diner's Club

Account #_____

Exp. Date_____

Signature_____

NAME _____

INSTITUTION _____

ADDRESS _____

CITY _____

STATE/ZIP _____

COUNTRY _____ COUNTY (NY residents only) _____

TEL _____ FAX _____

E-MAIL_____
May we use your e-mail address for confirmations and other types of information? ☐ Yes ☐ No

Order From Your Local Bookstore or Directly From
The Haworth Press, Inc.
10 Alice Street, Binghamton, New York 13904-1580 • USA
TELEPHONE: 1-800-HAWORTH (1-800-429-6784) / Outside US/Canada: (607) 722-5857
FAX: 1-800-895-0582 / Outside US/Canada: (607) 772-6362
E-mail: getinfo@haworthpressinc.com
PLEASE PHOTOCOPY THIS FORM FOR YOUR PERSONAL USE.

BOF96